CW00972361

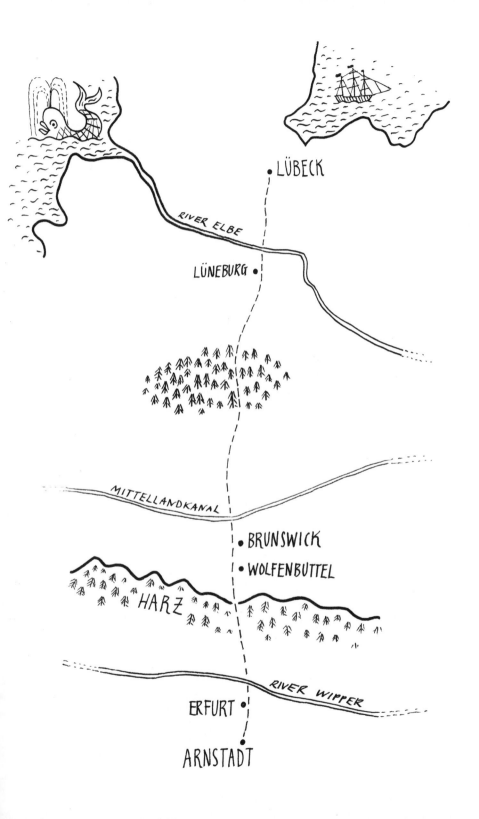

Published by Little Toller Books in 2018
Lower Dairy, Toller Fratrum, Dorset

Typeset in Garamond by Little Toller Books

Printed by TJ International Ltd, Padstow, Cornwall

All papers used by Little Toller Books are natural, recyclable products made from wood grown in sustainable, well-managed forests

A catalogue record for this book is available from the British Library

ISBN 978-1-908213-64-8

SOMETHING OF HIS ART

Walking to Lübeck with J. S. Bach

HORATIO CLARE

LITTLE TOLLER

To John Clare,
with love and deepest thanks for all the books, art, music and ideas
he has always shared with me, so kindly and so thoughtfully.
Thank you, dearest Dad.

Contents

At a certain moment here in Arnstadt he had so strong an urge to hear as many good organists as he could that he set out for Lübeck, on foot, in order to hear the famous organist of St Mary's, Dieterich Buxtehude. He stayed there not without benefit for almost quarter of a year, and then turned back to Arnstadt.

Emanuel Bach's obituary for his father

Once upon a time
in an organ loft

In the market square at Arnstadt in Thuringia, southern Germany, a young man lolls on his plinth, shirt open, legs apart, hands poised as though he plays an invisible lute. He might be in a tavern or resting on a bench. He is surely in company, his head raised for a response. The sculptor has imbued him with confidence, even arrogance; there is a lusty set to the splayed legs and the shirt open to the breastbone, a look that might be a provocation in the face. It seems a fair impression of Johann Sebastian Bach, aged twenty in the year 1705, given what we know of him.

Aged eighteen, in June 1703, he had been brought from Weimar to inspect the organ in Arnstadt's Neue Kirche. The church stands in the corner of the square – his statue can see it, slightly to the right of the town hall. Alighting from the carriage which the consistory of Arnstadt had sent for him, the young man was aware that he was under assessment as much as was the organ.

It was a prestigious commission for one so young, but the Bachs were used to this: as musicians of standing in the area, their livelihoods depended on the securing and fulfilling of commissions to write, inspect and perform. (Bach's elder brother Christoph had inspected the organ at Ohrdruf at the age of nineteen and given the builder a poor report.) The first time he walked into the Neue Kirche, Johann Sebastian must have been jumpy with anticipation, but one doubts he showed it. The family would not have thought of themselves as engaged in anything so crude as show business, but they knew all about performance.

The evaluation of an organ was no small thing: this one had cost Arnstadt about 800 florins. Few machines were more sophisticated at the turn of the eighteenth century. None spoke more clearly of a community's prestige. In the Neue Kirche the young inspector looked for any sign that the builder, the respected J. F. Wender, had stinted. He measured the air pressure and the thickness of the pipes. One trick was to pull out all twenty-three stops and play. If any of the inaccessible pipes were tin, rather than the more expensive lead, he would hear false notes. His son, Carl Philipp Emanuel, would later record Bach's method of measuring an organ's 'lungs', no doubt taught him by Christoph: 'To find out, he would draw out every speaking stop, and play in the fullest and richest possible texture. At this the organ builders would often grow quite pale with fright.' The Neue Kirche's organ passed, and the inspector, too. Bach was offered an excellent salary – fifty guilders, plus thirty thalers board and lodging – and established in Arnstadt as organist and cantor.

The church, his church, as he must have thought of it, remains sturdy and uninspiring on the outside. The Neue Kirche was then only twenty years old, its predecessor having burned down. Inside, it is unexpectedly lovely, light-filled Baroque with three galleries and a plain and sweetly curving barrel of a roof, the wooden interior painted in Reformation white.

I nip up to the organ loft while the lady in charge is explaining that the church is currently closed to visitors. The organ has been replaced several times, but you can feel the intimacy and privilege of being high up in a restricted space, with the smell of wood and metal, and the whole church below you like a breath inhaled, waiting for the notes of a chorale.

Outside it is a lovely morning, as fair as the little summer of Saint Martin, the day glowing on the cusp of October and November. A few months ago, Radio 3 asked me to follow in Bach's footsteps, tracing the journey he made on foot from here to Lübeck in the autumn of 1705. The production team cannot be spared for many days: we will walk sections of Bach's route, covering in less than a week a distance he must have done in under a month. Richard Andrews, the sound recordist, is lurking outside, microphones protruding from his backpack. Lindsay Kemp, the producer, is being sweetly diplomatic with the guardian lady. A gentle intellectual with thin but probably charming German, he wins her over. My spirits are alight and a-leap with the adventure we are embarked upon. I am thrilled to be so soon so close to Bach's shade.

★

Even without the statue, the church and square are busy with the young man's deeds and attitudes. Up here, to the choir gallery, he brings a mysterious 'unauthorised maiden', a girl whom he allows to sing with the choristers, in breach of regulations. She may or may not be his future wife, Maria Barbara. (The statue's visitors have perhaps unwittingly added a visual reference to the suggestions surrounding the incident by rubbing the bulge in Bach's crotch, brightening it from green to bright bronze.) Down there in the square, in front of the market hall, the young organist is involved in an infamous brawl. On the evening of August 4, 1705, he is set upon by one Johann Heinrich Geyersbach, who has been drinking at a christening party. Supported by five friends, Geyersbach, a musician, accosts Bach, demands an apology for a slight, and strikes the organist in the face with a cudgel. Bach draws his rapier and fights Geyersbach off. The latter will produce a shirt with holes in it and claim that Bach stabbed him. The complaint will go nowhere. It will be established that Bach had called him a *zippel Fagottist* ['a prick of a bassoonist'], publicly humiliating the older man. Bach will be reprimanded, Geyersbach let off: the incident will deepen Bach's irritation and estrangement from the authorities, who are already unhappy with their organist.

There have been complaints about him. Why will he not perform ensemble pieces with the student singers and players? Bach says he requires a 'competent' musical director; the inference is clear. Also, he has been making 'many odd variations' in the hymns, mixing in 'many strange keys' and confusing the congregation. One can imagine his expression when this is put to him: a carefully blank almost-absence of mockery. The written summary of his replies to his consistory overseers suggests he was laconic, prideful and obtuse by turns, just short of outright rudeness. These tiresome old fools, he thinks. The mixture of hauteur, insecurity and ambition in him is easy to imagine. He knows he has talent, perhaps enormous talent, but he cannot yet tell if the world will thwart its fulfilment. His solution will always be hard work – he will say, later, that any who worked as he had would succeed as he had – but a musician's work comes in many forms. Study, practice, listening, talking.

When he asks for four weeks leave in October 1705 it is granted, perhaps with some relief, by his supervisor. But as he sets out for Lübeck, 230 miles away, Bach must know that he will not be back for months. He installs Johann Ernst, his cousin, to perform his duties for him, packs a bag, and sets out.

He is going to seek Dieterich Buxtehude, organist and musical director at the Marienkirche in the free imperial city of Lübeck. He wants to learn – 'to comprehend one thing and another about his art' is the only explanation that has come down to us, given to the consistory court in Arnstadt, when he was asked to explain himself on his return, doing so with cryptic self-possession. Buxtehude is famous, the most exciting performer of the time. Lübeck allows him a latitude and freedom unknown in Thuringia. The influence of the music of the Italian Catholic church is much greater in the cosmopolitan north of the Holy Roman Empire than in the provincial south, the works of Monteverdi, Grandi and Carissimi, in John Eliot Gardiner's phrase, 'acting as a blood transfusion to the music of the Lutheran church'. Bach must have heard that Buxtehude's performances ranged from huge concerts, with ranks of musicians installed in galleries high up in Lübeck's Marienkirche, to deeply intimate and devotional chamber music. The great southern German organist Johann Pachelbel, Bach's brother Christoph's tutor, sent his own son, Wilhelm, to Buxtehude. George Frideric Handel and Johann Mattheson have been to see him: Buxtehude has inaugurated a series of evening concerts, *Abendmusiken*, which are drawing crowds of musicians and the musical. The concerts run on Sunday evenings in Advent: if Bach is to hear them, he must go now. And Buxtehude is old, verging on retirement. Does Bach dream of becoming his assistant? Of working with him, even taking over his job? It would be strange if he did not.

The young man is a seething of energy, talent and curiosity. *I know I am good but do not know how good or even if I will be allowed to find out...* He must have looked on Arnstadt as a stepping stone even as he finished inspecting their organ and they offered him the post. A fine machine, a good salary, he must have thought, but how quickly will I be able to move on? In everything we know of him at this time, from the insult to the improvisation, is impatience. Arnstadt, then as now, is a small and worthy town. After Weimar, where he had spent seven months, and Lüneburg, where he studied for two years from the age of fifteen, Arnstadt is a dull pond. He has been taught theology, musical theory, Latin, Greek, French and Italian; he can play the harpsichord, clavichord, violin and organ. No wonder banging out the same old hymns for a provincial congregation provokes him to improvise and play around. He is straining to stretch himself.

The mission to Buxtehude will be transformative, he hopes. It will be a journey through a string of towns and statelets, from Thuringia to Saxony-Anhalt to Lower Saxony to Schleswig-Holstein, in his time a mosaic of duchies. It will be the first time he has directed his own destiny without consulting family or employers. His way runs behind the church, across what is now a park, and then north along the River Gera. His first destination is Erfurt, where Pachelbel had established himself as organist, teacher and composer, instructing Christoph there when Bach was still a toddler. He surely made an early start.

The expedition was a pilgrimage of a sort, a pilgrimage for his art of a kind that was common in European culture then: the wandering scholar and the itinerant musician were both familiar figures, and cherished in Germany, where the need of young craftsmen to travel in order to learn from older masters was understood and respected. Perhaps every long-distance walk is a pilgrimage, whether the walker is a believer or not. The reconnection with ourselves through immersion in the world is inevitably therapeutic, and the deeper pleasure comes from a counterpoint: the similarity of each day in their greater rhythms and the diversity of each moment. Our walk is a pilgrimage, too. In following what we know and can guess of his footsteps, we hope to draw as close to that young man as it is possible to do across three centuries. It will change us in some of the same degrees it changed him; we will be fitter, more springy, our eyes refreshed, our horizons expanded and our internal landscapes renewed. Despite the years between us we will see and feel much of the same world that Bach did; under the same horizons we will encounter the same paths, trees, plants, birds and animals. We will be crossing one of the most fascinating and perhaps the most significant of modern European states.

My daily progress will be a peculiar blend of solitude and company. Richard and Lindsay walk some way behind me so that my microphone does not register their presence, Richard recording his footsteps, which will be used instead of mine, and both of them listening to whatever narration I come up with. Lindsay, who has scouted the route and who will cut days of material down to five programmes, carries the map. My task is easy: to think aloud on Bach, landscape, people and place, which for me is the perfect commission. The heaviest burden is Richard's: he is carrying recording equipment and microphones on a pole, harnessed in a wooden frame of his own invention, which allows him to gather the atmospheres and natural sounds we encounter. Richard is an amused and phlegmatic man with several lives – sound engineer, musician and performer. We both mock Lindsay, because he is the sort of good-natured, gentle person who says things like, 'I took a pen from that hotel when I was here doing the recce. I meant to put it back but I've taken another one by mistake.'

★

It is a perfect day for walking out of Arnstadt's colours, the roofs red, the buildings yellow and green, the cobbled streets falling towards the Gera. The lime trees are still in leaf, dappling the shade under fine high cloud. What joy there is in setting out on a proper walk! You want to greet everyone you meet; your untried step has a swing in it and your pack is light on your back.

What did Bach take with him? We know he went armed. German students were permitted to wear rapiers on their journeys to university. They carried their term's fees in cash, and so were allowed to defend themselves from robbers. Germany's student body were a boisterous and unruly class in this period, confrontational, riotous, swaggering about with swords and affronting authority, which was a severe and humourless presence. Merely insulting another citizen was punishable by fines and a month's imprisonment. Perhaps the young, discontented and rebellious, felt they had inherited restriction, privation and uncertainty in the aftermath of the Thirty Years' War. Its legacy lay heavy across the land and psyche of the Holy Roman Empire. Their elders had seen horrors, and now lived in a convoluted system of tradition, regulation and hierarchy in a dying empire. The Peace of Westphalia held sway, but Hanover, Saxony, Prussia, Sweden and Russia were fighting the Great Northern War in what are now Poland and Lithuania. The scourge of the Thirty Years' War was half a century old, but the emancipation of the peasantry was yet to come.

Although Bach's life would overlap theirs, he was decades in advance of Kant, Goethe and Schiller, a Baroque outrider before the Enlightenment. He was walking out of the grip of small-town mores into a countryside still in recovery from war, plague and starvation. Thuringia, his homeland, retained much of its great forest, but the woods were unmanaged: traditional systems overturned by war were still in disarray, the lives of the populace insecure.

Self-containment must have been natural to him, an orphan since the age of nine. He would have taken enough money for a long absence. A leather knapsack of some sort would be obvious, containing a change of clothes, no doubt, perhaps a woollen cloak against the weather, surely a pen, and maybe manuscript paper for composition – which was valuable and would have needed protecting from the rain. No doubt he took a good walking stick, against dogs.

And he never travelled quite alone. 'Where there is devotional music, God with his grace is always present,' he wrote in the margins of a Bible commentary. Bach's ambition was not limited to himself and his music; he had been raised in a Lutheran home, sung Luther's hymns and absorbed his theology from infancy (and studied in the same Latin School in Eisenach). Luther was adamant on the role of music – 'the notes make the words live'. A composer and performer such as Bach gave breath to the word of God; there was always a higher purpose, alongside, beneath and beyond his worldly concerns. No artist of any worth ever works without one, whether or not he or she is religious.

The River Gera takes us north, a fat and busy brook, embanked, lined with a footpath and a cyclepath. Everywhere is evidence of municipal spending: the cycle-

and footpaths are generous and immaculate; the trees all sport nest boxes, each numbered. At first, there are few birds. Blackbirds alarm at our passing and chaffinches sing. The nest boxes seem very hopeful, but sadly too clean to have been much used, as if the municipality has provided shelter and a numbered address for the entire local population, who have either disdained them or, dread thought, are simply too few to take advantage.

We set off too quickly, over-keen to get going, to make miles. Bach must have paced himself. In a society and an age when long-distance walking was quotidian, he would have been joining a steady flow of other travellers, and none of those on foot would have gone with avoidable haste. Haste means rubs and blisters, unreasonable stress on your boots; it robs the journey of a slice of its pleasures, and Bach already knew about travel. Just before his fifteenth birthday he had left his school in Ohrdruf with his friend Georg Erdmann and set out on a necessary but surely rich adventure. Their scholarship fund at Ohrdruf having run out, the boys journeyed over 200 miles to take up posts as choristers in Lüneburg. Bach's inspiration for this Lübeck journey five years later was with him on that venture, too: he carried a transcription of a chorale fantasia by Buxtehude to Lüneburg, probably copied out under his brother's supervision; the manuscript is spotted with raindrops.

So, as he sets out, he knows something of what the road will hold: he takes it with no huge rush, but does not linger much, either. Whatever time he had away he meant to use. Buxtehude did not know he was coming; who knew in what state he would find the master?

It was a direct and purposeful walker who settled into

his stride beside the north-running Gera, on the way to Erfurt. He knew the road well: Bachs had lived and moved between Arnstadt and Erfurt for generations. His grandfather Christoph, his father Ambrosius and his uncle Christoph all lived in Erfurt and played in the town band. On this familiar path, walking over ground long entwined with his family, their history and their contacts, perhaps his frustrations seemed close upon him. But they must have fallen away, paced out moment by moment, leavened by hope, change and stimulus. Perhaps he is recognised as he leaves town; perhaps he passes members of the congregation on the way. Good day, Herr Bach.

Goodbye...

There is such a freshness to this autumn day; 'a time when all that is good rejoices,' E. M. Forster wrote of September, in *A Room With A View*. The ash trees and hazels are turned and shedding, there are four inches of fallen leaves underfoot, summer's burned plans, and a huge grey heron sweeps over the river. The poplars are magnificent, a line of trees brushed like a giant jump hedge, entirely bare like witches' brooms, echoing the sweeps of the mares' tails, the high alto-cirrus in the blue above them. What fillips of sudden joy he must have experienced on his way. He knew the rushing intensity of utmost joy. I listen to Cantata 51 again and again – *Praise God in every land!* The aria, a dance between soprano and trumpet, sings of a God of spiralling ascension, a towering whirl of praise, fragility made might. There is such play and lightness in it, as though the act of praising is itself the soul of joy, shot through with humour, with a teasing self-deprecation in the nimble delicacy of the melody, the effect both humble and exalting. *All the creatures of earth and sky exalt his glory...* Yes, yes! What is glory if not multiplicity, if not detail in infinity, if not a flock of birds?

The songs of the morning are various, as we walk along the river. The soundscape can have altered little in centuries. Between Bruegel, a hundred and fifty years earlier, and Constable, a hundred later, there is no change in the noise you can hear in the paintings. There were so many birds, then. Bruegel has them on every bush and tree. There must have been volleys of finches, sparrows, thrushes and tits along Bach's path, and kingfishers by the river, and waterfowl. Dogs' barks and the hoofbeats of horses ring through eighteenth-century landscape painting. The countryside would have been far more animated and peopled, alive sometimes with voices you could hear a field away – though in the agrarian parts of the world now it is noticeable that the pickers and viticulturists of Europe, the herdsmen of Africa and the planters of China make little noise as they work.

The gardens of the suburbs of Arnstadt speak of so many lives, with their spacious lawns, children's toys, trampolines and Wendy houses. Some of the toys and dens are long disused; the owners have outgrown them, or they belong to grandparents not much visited. The backs of houses give way to paddocks where brown and white skewbald horses come to investigate us, nuzzling towards the furry Rycote windshield on Richard's microphone. He makes as if to interview them and they offer no comment but soft breathing. There is something quietly and utterly tender in the way horses sometimes stand close to one another, with less than a horse's width between them. No wonder children love them.

The riverside is easy walking; a bridge takes us to woodland, the path becomes the raised ghost of a railway line leading us on through small villages: Ichtershausen, Eischleben. The conurbations fall away and huge Thuringian skies cloud slowly, rays of sun lighting distant hills. Under bridges is graffiti – FICK DIE AFD ('Stuff Alternative für Deutschland') is a common sentiment, AfD being the populist anti-immigrant party, which does ever better in elections, particularly here in the old East Germany.

(Hateful as swastikas are, I would rather see them scrawled out under bridges than graffiti like this with which I agree. You do not want those holding kind, enlightened views to be relegated to the spray-canned dank underpasses and tunnels, where fascists and bigots belong.)

Into farmland now, we pass a knotted region, tireless and tiring with motorways. Bullocks flap their ears at us and wind turbines turn below the horizons, their blades flashing over the near skylines of huge, undulating fields, green-blue with nitrogen. We meet a lady with a Labrador the same colour as her hair, and a farmer, amused, who wants to know what we are doing. Lindsay's answer delights him, but whether this is down to the content or the addled German form of the explanation is hard to say. As the path takes us away from the roads, into an airy afternoon and a lightly wooded region, the cry of the green woodpecker, the rainbird, yaffles through the thickening air. There is a nuthatch, my favourite woodland bird, the male impeccably dressed as if for the races, in tones of grey-blue and yellow silk. The species count is rising gently and I am vigilant, delighted at every sign of life. Germany has reported catastrophic falls in numbers of insects: in German nature reserves there has been 75 per cent fall over the last twenty-five years. 75 per cent! Like the loss of sea-ice, like the towering rate of the extinction of species, there are some statistics at which you reel internally in a kind of denying numbness before you move swiftly and guiltily on, like the perpetrator of a crime. It is done. What can I do? One sign of hope is the banning of neonicotinoid pesticides. Manufactured by a German company, Bayer AG, they have recently been banned by the European Union. Their withdrawal is a recognition that every bee, moth and fly, every living creature matters now, their abundance a memory that has been fading with every generation. Bach's way must have been tinily turbulent with ants, beetles, flies and midges, even so late in the year, and with all the birds that fed on them.

The hedgeless, unfenced fields are not quite empty of life, but they are only the demesnes of crows and magpies, ragged emperors of emptiness. In the distance are villages with onion-domed churches; we hear bells at midday from the Catholic spires, while the Protestant churches are quiet; in both, the architectures of the ages of faith are perfectly maintained, but they are somehow doleful, infrequently used.

We lunch on sausage and bread and break off in the churchyard at Molsdorf, laying down our packs, easing our feet.

'What do you think he ate?' I ask Lindsay.

'This, probably,' Lindsay says. 'Nice bit of bratwurst.'

'And apples?'

'Lots around at the moment,' Lindsay says.

The orchards we pass are abundant, fruit lying in the long grass, picked over by blackbirds looking for grubs. He would not have needed to carry water; there would have been inns, wells and stopping places for travellers along the road. As the historian Helmut Walser Smith points out, the experience of travel through German lands at the beginning of the eighteenth century was changing, but little was written about it. 'Until the early 1770s there were virtually no extended musings about the beautiful countryside, no appreciative hymns to the rural world, and no sympathetic musings on the peasantry,' Smith writes. The discovery of landscape and place as literary subjects was still to come, but journeying through them was increasingly straightforward. Maps showing roads and settlements were being printed in the cities and widely distributed. Although Bach's way was a venerable south–north route, almost certainly marked with milestones, he would have been able to purchase local maps of the stages of his journey from itinerant map-sellers. The documents were also available through the mail, which was well organised, with hundreds of postal stations across the country, 900 of them by 1760. The well-off travelled by coach; Bach would have passed a great many on his way. His natural walking day would have accorded with the light: although the great cities were erecting oil lamps to illuminate public spaces around this time, many smaller provincial towns would not light up until the end of the eighteenth century, and not until after the Napoleonic Wars in some areas. Helmut Walser Smith tells the story of a contemporary traveller, Zacharias Konrad von Uffenbach, who journeyed through Lower Saxony on his way to England in 1704. 'He noted inventions, from massive cranes, to especially delicate weighing scales, to tiny mathematical instruments.' Crossing Bach's path in the preceding year, Uffenbach gives an impression of a society advancing on all scales, from macro to then micro technology.

The afternoon lengthens and the light ages, gilding again as we link the villages, passing Möbisburg, travelling from one dog-walking circuit to another along paths which feel as though they are much exercised and thought over. Travellers later in the century record that many of the rural populace still lived in huts with roofs of straw. What Bach saw of these quiet villages would not have changed in hundreds of years.

The creak of cartwheels, the tread of horses and the tock of woodcutters' axes must have accompanied our walker. The mind cycles between periods of rest and observation, when the present unscrolls in sense impressions, the world passing to the rhythm of the feet, and periods of busy thought and activity, when the gaze disengages from the thoughts, finding a kind of part-seeing neutral, and the attention turns inwards. Songs, hymns, chorales and cantatas, including perhaps the beginnings of what became his first, *Nach dir, Herr, verlanget mich* (Cantata BWV* 150), were his to hear or sing at will. *For you, Lord, is my longing* was not written by a happy man. At the outset there is a slow heaviness in its careful pacing, something like the weight of depression,

---

* BWV refers to Bach-Werke-Verzeichnis, a catalogue of Bach's compositions, edited by Wolfgang Schmieder, first published in 1950.

a young man's frustration, perhaps, before the words of Psalm 25 are given: *My God, I hope* (long-drawn-out 'hope') *in you; Let me not be put to shame, to shame, to shame... so that my enemies may not rejoice over me.* A young man's sentiments, surely, with all his dwelling on shame and enemies. The cantata includes parts for bassoon, including, as John Eliot Gardiner observes, 'a fast passage covering a range of two octaves and a minor third – playable by a competent professional but not by a student sight-reading, let alone a *zippel Fagottist*. Had Bach placed the perfect banana skin and engineered a final public showdown with his nemesis?' Gardiner asks.

What slights and put-downs, what conflicts and cornerings did he think about in those early hours and days? He was free from the thumping anxiety of emptiness, anyway. The huge privilege of an educated mind and much trained memory is recalled by George Orwell in his essay 'The Spike': 'I have come to think that boredom is the worst of all a tramp's evils, worse than hunger and discomfort, worse even than the constant feeling of being socially disgraced. It is a silly piece of cruelty to confine an ignorant man all day with nothing to do; it is like chaining a dog in a barrel. Only an educated man, who has consolations within himself, can endure confinement.'

Bach on his walk cannot have been bored for many moments. While being a passenger breeds a passive blankness, walking never quite does. There are always longueurs in a day's peregrination, and we stride through them as the horizons heave up wind turbines and the heavy skies withhold colour, but Bach was surely able to sing, hum or compose as he wished.

Autumn's smells would have come sudden and strong to him, as they do now, that rich biscuit scent of sweetness and decay from tangled undergrowth which looks as though it never quite dries.

As the afternoon tips towards evening, the air blues and birds begin to move, chaffinches, long-tailed tits and wood pigeons shifting around us. It is that softly marvellous time of day when the heart lifts at the setting sun and the colours gently flare. We pass a farming family busy among their fruit trees. These people are collectors, the way some farmers are; the ground around their home supports apple and pear trees, geese, chickens, horses, dogs, and all in immaculate order, no hint of sprawl or mess. We exchange nods and greetings.

Who did Bach talk to on his way? There would have been farmers, merchants and peasants on the road, and hunters in the woods. If he met a fellow musician he would have been tempted to say something. Did he fall into conversation, or hold himself apart? He must have been asked where he was going – on any foot journey someone is bound to enquire. To Lübeck, he surely said, but did he ever say why? Perhaps only another musician would have understood. Hold-ups, river crossings, tolls and exceptional weather tend to bunch travellers and set them talking. His youth, purpose and ambition would have given him a containment and confidence that did not need conversation to bolster it, but towards the end of the days and at his night stops he would have been ready for some human exchange. No one walks so far in silence.

There are buds on the hazel bushes. The first catkins, tightly rolled pink scrolls, promise spring beyond the coming winter. Bischleben appears as a white Lego stickle of buildings in the distance, a tower on the side of a hill above the river valley. Lindsay and Richard turn back here, the day's recording done, but I press on into Erfurt, cheating, taking the commuter train, for the sake of arriving in the city as Bach must have done – having surely started earlier – at evening, as the lights and lamps came up.

Coming into a town as night falls is a wonderful feeling after a day's walk. You move through the streets, your eyes sharpened by the length of the day's views, your feet tired and your muscles worked, alert and fatigued at once. In a broad square there is a demonstration against the AfD, in favour of immigration and in solidarity with immigrants. Students and left-wing campaigners are listening to a speaker and handing out leaflets.

On the evening that Bach walked into town, Erfurt's concern would not have been overpopulation but its opposite. The city had known great prosperity in previous centuries: a centre of woad production, and a major hub on the Via Regia, the Holy Roman Empire's principal west–east trade route – running from France to Russia, if you followed it far enough, and locally linking the Rhine at Frankfurt to the eastern river systems at Leipzig. Erfurt counted many blessings until the Thirty Years' War. When the conflict began, being on easy marching roads became a curse, and in the outbreaks of plague that came with and after the soldiers, being on a trade route was a fatal vulnerability. The plague spread particularly quickly along them.

The idea of driving away incomers in 1705 would have seemed absurd. Thuringia lost a third of its population to war and plague. Trade southwards to Italy had shrivelled: economic power was accruing in the north, around the old Hanseatic cities. Bach's destination, Lübeck, had been a free city since 1226, and was perfectly positioned to take advantage of the new axis, once the Great Northern War was over. Bach was walking out of the forest lands and ways of life of an older time, towards the brightening lights. All the same, Erfurt on an autumn evening in 1705 would have been busy and lively, the harvest recently in, farmers, merchants and traders packing the market squares. I choose the oldest Gasthaus I can find and eat and drink, looking at the broad, healthy faces of Thuringia. Big-boned and fair-haired, perhaps many of them carry the genes descended from the Danish and Swedish armies which swept or limped through the region during the Thirty Years' War.

The venerable streets behind the cathedral have not changed since that time; the cobbles are as they were and the turn and press of the buildings is the same. Instead of taverns there are now cocktail bars. Where they would have been busy with the drawing down of Bach's day, this evening they are yet quiet: we go out later than our ancestors. Even while still in recovery from the depopulations of the plague, Erfurt was a far richer and more stimulating place than Arnstadt. Erfurt's old fish market, where north–south and east–west trade routes intersected, made such a mark on the town that its name is retained: a very lively centre in Bach's time, then, offering fresher fayre than he could have ordered in Arnstadt. Soup and fish for Johann Sebastian is my guess, and I order the same thing.

Embarked as he was on his pilgrimage, Bach, I fancy, would have kept to himself, arranging his own lodgings, but the young walker would surely have had options for accommodation through contacts here. His father, Ambrosius, had been appointed into Erfurt's company of musicians in 1667. Here in 1668, he married Bach's mother, Elisabeth Lammerhirt, the daughter of a town councillor. That family were in the fur trade, successful and entwined in the town's affairs; no doubt Ambrosius and Elisabeth retained many ties here after their move to Eisenach, where Bach was born in 1685. After thirteen years in Eisenach, Ambrosius would request that he be allowed to return to Erfurt, but he was a very popular musician, head town piper, and the court of Duke Johann Georg I at Eisenach declined to release him.

So if he ate alone that night in Erfurt, Bach must have mulled on his family, and his memories of his father who had died when he was ten. He must have had an air about him, sitting alone and slightly apart.

The best portrait of Ambrosius's son, by Elias Gottlob Haussmann in 1746, completed in Leipzig when Bach was sixty-one, shows a man of absolute self-certainty. Bewigged, quietly but expensively dressed in blue velvet, fleshy with good health and an evident appetite for food and drink, he has the gaze of one accustomed to being looked at. The dark eyes are bright and stern and certainly not humourless. There is quick, tough wit there, along with a look that is partly inward, as though Bach is a very rapid listener, used to considering what he hears before most speakers have finished. In those eyes, which are not symmetrical, is a man who jumps ahead of his interlocutors, ever retaining his own internal conversation. He does not look as though he needs anyone or anything.

Some of that certainty and much of the fixity of purpose is already his tonight, reinforced by his first day of walking. In the portrait he holds a sheet of music, a three-part fragment to the painting's viewer, but from the perspective of the sitter, once the music is reversed and read from his point of view (back to front, from ours), a canon in six parts. He can never have been without a piece he was working upon – never without music within music, the visual puzzle and pun in the portrait suggests – either in manuscript or in his head. If there were instruments being played in the streets and inns around the cathedral he surely paused to listen. John Eliot Gardiner describes Bach's music as 'dance-impregnated', the zest and joy of it, to his ear, at odds with a mincing, English 'holy holy' approach to the Great Man's work. I wonder what he had come up with, that first day of low horizons, distant views, woods and birds, on the northward road.

The Harz

For the next few days, Johann Sebastian Bach walked north through Thuringia. The season was on the turn, autumn's colours brightening, the leaf-fall thickening, the skies offering a little more rain than they do on our dry walk, perhaps. But 1705 was not a wet year, with the exception of a fierce storm in the Channel in August, so it seems reasonable to assume that in early November Bach was not often soaked or detained by heavy weather. The way was easy-going, the slow heaves of the Thuringian contours offering gentle ascents and steady downhill paths. The forest, which was so much part of his Thuringian identity and the region's culture, has been felled, only remnants enduring on ridges to the west of Bach's route. He would have seen cranes migrating. We watch them, a thrilling, flickering line resolving as they draw near us into a flock of fifty birds. They are bearing south-east, a languid and exalting sight as they seem to tow one another through the cool high air, sailing through the sea of the sky.

If he kept a steady pace, fifteen to twenty miles a day, the fifth or sixth day of his walk would have found him in the foothills of the Harz mountains. We do not know his exact route. Between Arnstadt and Lübeck, elements of his way are all but certain: the direct and much-used ways run from Arnstadt north to Erfurt, from Brunswick (Braunschweig) to Lüneburg, and Lüneburg to Lübeck. How he dealt with the Harz is the central ambiguity of his journey. Going east would have been senseless, adding a week for no reason. To circle the mountains on the western side would have added three or four days walking, while heading straight over would have been swifter work, if initially more taxing. We decide to investigate the possibility that speed, variation in landscape and the stimulation of the legends and mysteries of the Harz drew Bach to the high ground. He had never been into the mountains, though he must have seen them on his travels to and from Lüneburg. Why not take the opportunity to cross them? They were ever an attractive range to walkers and travellers. In 1799, Coleridge would make three journeys to the highest peak in the range, Brocken. 'Woods crowding upon woods, hills over hills,' he wrote, noting the hollow sound of birdsong among the fir trees of 'sov'ran Brocken, woods and woody Hills.'

The striking fact of the Harz is that they are not mountains at all, but high ridged hills with the Brocken summit their central peak. Their folds rise in steep slopes, thickly forested with conifers. The frequent mists make an eerily atmospheric island of high ground rising above

the Thuringian basin to the south and the fair lands of
Saxony to the north. As in the Tyrol, the brooding and
introverted silences of the forest, the way the trees seem
to lean in and listen, the dim impenetrable under-spaces
where nothing grows and the sudden bright glades
amid the pines fed the natural tendency of hill people
to populate their forests with spirits. While the Tyrol
abounds with fairy folk, trolls and dragons, the Harz
belong to witches.

A century after Bach's walk, Goethe set his
Walpurgis night scene on the Brocken, where Faust
and Mephistopheles watch witches disporting with the
devil. Goethe's descriptions of ancient ribs of granite
rock, uprooted trees, murky vapours and abyssal
falls – culled from his three ascents of the Harz, the
first in 1777 – are typically accurate, but a dramatic
condensation of the actual landscape. The Harz present
no great obstacle to the walker.

The ways up the valleys and over the ridges must have
been much busier in Bach's time than they are now, when
driving around them is easy and walking a mere pastime.
Then, the mountains rang with industry: copper, lead,
iron, zinc and especially silver were mined here from
the Middle Ages onwards. To the north, the Duchies
of Brunswick, Wolfenbüttel and Lüneburg grew rich on
Harz silver. (Deep under the trees, the riddles of tunnels
are still here. During the Cold War, when this was the
westernmost outpost of the Soviet military, there were
rumours of secret ways under the Iron Curtain through
the mines.) A traveller in 1705 would have seen many
more people on the tracks than do we, and heard more
of their doings, too. Rocks and ores were quarried with

gunpowder from the early seventeenth century onwards, with water pumps and extensive drainage tunnels deployed to keep the mines operable.

On a still mountain morning, seven buzzards circling in a thermal above us and the air sweet with dew, we begin to climb. The going is soft, cushioned with pine needles underfoot. Bright moss animates the granite tors and every grade and form of conifer tree seems to waddle towards us, from foot-high saplings to towering fifty-footers. The woods are wonderfully scented with the held-in cool smell of silver birch and the intoxicating Christmas reek of the conifers. Bach would have been entirely adapted to the walking now, his body conformed to the activity, his legs loose and his feet springy. His way would have been more interesting, botanically, with the remnants of the original Harz forest of beech trees far richer and more beautiful to walk through than the current dominant monoculture of Norway spruce.

Our soundscape is suddenly his, as clouds like smoke and ashes drift over the tree-tops and we pass bands of small birds: coal tits, hawfinches, crossbills and goldcrests. They occur together in charms, safety and song in numbers, suddenly animating a stretch of track, a stand of trees, the hillside, the whole morning. What an intensely, existentially lonely and empty world this would be, bereft of birds. And what a vivid, flourished, life-detailed planet it is, in their presence. The Harz mountains advertise lynx, owls and capercaillies, all reintroduced, though there would have been plenty of them in Bach's time. The last bear was killed on the Brocken in the year of his walk. The last wolves survived until the end of the century but began to settle back in the Harz a couple of years ago.

The destruction of the environment seems particularly to belong to us now, as if we stand at an apex of hapless vandalism, as if our species and we as individuals, so numerous and so demanding, cannot help but lay waste to other species and the planet. But it is heartening, in a strange way, that we have destroyed before, and restored before. If Bach did walk through the Harz he would have noted the general destruction of the high hardwoods, which were being coppiced and burned for charcoal, a process which had become voracious around 1700. Two years after his journey, strangers without special permission were banned from the Brocken and fire-lighting was prohibited. In 1718, it was ordered that any form of destruction or damage to the forest would be punished. Although forestry, mining and hunting continued to denude the hills for the next two centuries, the last hundred years have brought a dazzling resurgence: well managed – even given the Norway spruce – protected and enriched with reintroductions, the mountains are now almost as alive as ever they were.

'Are there bears?' I ask a forester with a massive 4x4, just for fun.

'Lynx,' he says, with satisfaction.

A gypsy caravan carrying children passes us, cart horses with hoofs like dinner plates trotting with clop and jingle. Huge, heavy ravens like dinosaurs jump out of the top of spruce trees.

Richard complains that every time I identify a bird a different species calls. 'You say "goldcrest" and a raven shouts "*kark*"!' he moans. I am looking for nutcrackers amid the silver-pale of the trunks. The larches thin and suddenly there are ridges and valleys jagged with conifers falling away below us. The mist thickens and thins in skeins, keels of vapour sweeping across the track ahead and behind. At the top of the pass comes a moment of absolute certainty: the main route from south to north rises from Thuringia behind us, up to the crest in an easy day's stage, and descends to the border between Lower Saxony and Saxony-Anhalt in another day's stroll. Of course he came this way! All the mining activity would have guaranteed lodgings and food along the route; the landscape would have been as full of interest as any he had seen (he had not yet seen the sea) and he would have saved himself days and blisters.

As we rise, the mist closes in and steam trains hoot through the valleys, their cries swooping and spooky in the dimming silver of the cloud. The Harz are deeply haunted. During the Second World War thousands of slave labourers died in the mine tunnels, making V2 rockets. On the top of Brocken the mist darkens from silver to black, tall communications towers showing only their ankles in the cloud. Here is a large signboard, on which an image of breaking barbed wire frames a silhouette of Brocken's summit with its masts, commemorating the fall of the Berlin Wall in 1989 and the departure of the last Soviet troops in 1994. This is as far west as the Russians got, and it is the last place they left.

At the top, behind Germany's highest railway station, is a café serving currywurst, chips and beer under yellow lightbulbs, which cast a sheen of the 1950s. The hefty women working in the café are severe and grudging: they look as though they remember a Brocken and an internal border and a Stasi state that tourists like us could not possibly imagine. Our microphones and kit evidently do not endear us.

There are peculiar spirits abroad, as the dark and cold press against the windows; the exchanges of the Russian troops and border guards who were billeted here seemed to have caught in the fabric of the walls, I think, but perhaps it is all projection. The summit was a closed military zone until 1994. The fact that we are able to stroll past commemorative signs and pass without let or hindrance over the fence lines, where once we would have been shot, and order currywurst and beer where once conscripts ate in identical uniforms is all testament to and proof of German, European and human progress. Perhaps the ladies – whose memories, I would judge, are long and detailed – feel that we do not appreciate our good fortune. Perhaps we are just mouths on legs, as all tourists become, at some point, to those tired of serving them at the end of a long autumn day. It is surely coincidence, but the demographic one expects in mountain restaurants, the retired and fit, with their appropriate and expensive hiking gear, are absent. The only animation under the yellow lights comes from a mother, father and two children from France.

We descend through time on a steam train, hot and dim-lit and apparently existing in its own permanent war film. In these bewitched hills, all of time and history occur at once, it seems, and linger for centuries. The Harz contain deep seams of the German story, and we glimpse them, this cold autumn night: the stories many older Germans know and live with, that tourists may apprehend momentarily but never perhaps comprehend.

We lodge at the foot of the hills, in a 1970s concrete fantasia, the Hotel Maritim in Braunlage. Conditions for Johann Sebastian might be guessed at by the description that Coleridge gives of travelling through the same region later in the eighteenth century: the German love of soup (Coleridge tasted over twenty different kinds, he claimed), the styles of tobacco pipes – 'cane, clay porcelain, wood, tin, silver, and ivory' – the fantastic signboards above the shops, the enormous organs in the churches, and the inns, expensive (perhaps more so to foreigners, though Coleridge, in the aftermath of Waterloo, records the esteem in which Germans held the English) and offering brandy, bacon, coffee and, if you could afford no better, straw to sleep upon. The poet climbed Brocken three times, the second and third occasion back to back, at evening and on the following morning, in search of the Brocken Spectre. This is a giant cloud shadow cast by a walker standing between the sun and the mist which appears to halo the shadow's head with a circular rainbow known as a Glory. Coleridge found no spectre, but records that his efforts 'were amply repayed by the sight of a Wild Boar with an immense Cluster of Glow-worms round his Tail & Rump.'

The Woods

Bach's trail resumes on the plains of Lower Saxony, north of the Harz mountains. Beechwoods and fifty-acre fields soften under a gilding sun, the land descending from the mountains. A cousin of Bach's was *Kapellmeister* (chapel master) at Wolfenbüttel; his house would have made a good night stop. If the weather is on his side Bach is enjoying his walk. The land now is all invitation, as its contours would have been to Bach, at least. There are low hills to the west, lines of trees, riding stables, wind turbines still on the horizons and just enough movement in the air to deflect the leaves as they fall. Young beech trees, pines and triple-canopy woodland enfold the walker, the gentle rattle of wind moving the leaves sound quite different from the shushing of summer foliage.

There are oak trees with bird boxes above you as the path through the woods unrolls in perfect lengths of vision, offering enticement and variation, a series of hundred-metre strolls to the next dip or turn. While the plain of Thuringia is flat plates and upturned saucers, the fields of Lower Saxony feel different, smaller, an older layout of land. The declines in the contours have flattened and broadened, running north–south. Great tits and blue tits are abroad, coming close to investigate us then flitting away. Blue tits are the most remarkable disseminators of information: they pass news of threats from bird to bird across a wood in moments, so our passage is common knowledge in the Oderwald forest this morning. The soil is brown-grey clay, ideal for beech trees, and aromatic, the air filled with the sweet-rich smell of beech, which seems both green and brown. All over the land the light is lovely, a pearly glow of veiled sun which attaches light to surfaces, rather than bouncing it off them. Misty air rises from the ground as high cloud above us disperses. The path narrows to a boot's width, the beeches lined silver like elephants' legs. In the upper canopy their leaves are sprays of gold and russet. At our feet the ground is dug over by wild boar. The British press report that one in three of Saxony's boars is considered too radioactive to eat – a legacy of the Chernobyl nuclear disaster, over thirty years ago. Rather wonderfully, this does not seem to bother the boars, who are thriving. The track is turned and gored, excavated and scored, trotter-prints sunk deep in the humus. It is a morning like a song.

He must have composed as he walked, the pace of his stride setting a time signature. Out of contact with the world, freed of all responsibility, he must have moved in thought between memory and ambition, in and out of the vivid present, which would have been lit, as mine is, by the sudden appearance of goldcrests, rings of mushrooms and fungi, hawks and buzzards and all the denizens of the day.

Goldcrests are a particular wonder, atoms of pure life, their vivacity in marvellously inverse proportion to their tiny size. They animate the forest with an astonishing quality of suddenness, as though their lives are lived in another frame of time, quick, quick, pause, quick again, their notes so small and somehow curling, as though they slip miniature, perfect sound through weights of light and time and day made lumpen by their fragility. He noted them; he was a noticer, after all, as writers must be, and he hitched his pack and walked on. Did he carry books? The Bible perhaps, or commentaries. Theological scholarship was a necessity of his trade: he would need to write cantatas which accorded with the weekly sermons, so reading, memorising and note-taking would have been a natural part of his routine. In his copy of the Calov Bible (a three-volume Bible with commentary by Abraham Calovius which Bach owned and annotated), he marks a passage from Chronicles: 'They were to proclaim God's messages, accompanied by the music of harps and cymbals'. In the margin Bach writes, 'This chapter is the foundation of all God-pleasing church music.' How delighted and purposeful was the hand that held the underlining quill: his music was for the praise of God, it was praise; it was capable of praising and pleasing God.

A person of faith could not but see God in these woods on a day like this. You walk through rainbows of autumnal colour, jades, golds, opals and emerald.

A line of migrating cranes in a skein pass over, their conversation like voices, cymbals and trumpets.

In the later afternoon the woods begin to thin. Bach anticipates visiting his cousin; not far now, and all downhill. They will talk music and exchange family gossip; they will discuss Buxtehude and the walk. Bach will put his feet up and there will be a fire going. Perhaps his cousin produces some of his compositions and they discuss the finer points. As all writers, they will talk about who is composing what and for whom, and about where the good jobs and salaries are; they are bound to discuss organs, employers and consistories. At some point the incident with Geyersbach, the bassoonist, will come up. Bach will tell that story in a few dry sentences.

The view opens to clouds you would paint in white lead, grey and apricot, and to wide fields, a kind and rolling scape. The edge of the wood smells beautiful, a rich beechy must, as we follow four Dalmatians attached to three walkers, the dogs bouncing light on their feet. The gently busy bourgeoisie of Saxony look contented: the kind of people who wrote Bach's cheques and filled his pews taking their evening stroll. The way running ahead of us is dreamy now, a round-topped road under an avenue of young ash, with all the charm of a French lane under a Saxon sunset. Another tree line runs away into the distance and the route is unfenced, leading across a low hill with woods on one side and the sunset behind, the air silky as in the distance the clouds break, their crests illuminated. Overhead, the lid of cloud is a soft symphony in greys and blues, the texture of a river bottom upside down in the sky. How miraculous and how ordinary the evening is; how it passes, barely remarked, if at all, like so many millions, so many billions of evenings on our planet. You need music to speak of its wide peace, of its lingering, its uncounted and uncountable moments. Just over the brow, about two inches high, is the green spire of the Church of the Blessed Virgin at Wolfenbüttel; it was less than a century old, so copper, when Bach saw it. We walk under young oak, uplifted by the peace and order of a cultivated land intertwined with rich woodland, all sheltered under grand, wide skies. The day dims but the light brightens as the sun sinks below the lid. Down into the town we swing. Wolfenbüttel is quietly elegant, timber-framed buildings Bach would have recognised lining streets that wind around the Oker river. The town's main prize is the Herzog August Library. In Bach's time the largest library north of the Alps, its collections were miraculously preserved and protected from the devastation of the Thirty Years' War. When Bach passed it in 1705, the collection was under the care of Gottfried Leibniz. Leibniz was then engaged, alongside ground-breaking work on truth, calculus, topology and momentum, in inventing an indexing system for libraries.

A student couple are meandering into town, sharing a pair of ear-plug headphones.

'It's very boring,' says she, 'You have to go to Brunswick to do anything.'

'How come your English is so good?'

'We grew up with English on the radio,' he says.

'The American army radio stations had the best songs,' she explains.

In a thickening violet dusk the Marienkirche, the Church of the Blessed Virgin Mary, is lit from within, towering over its gardens where blackbirds chink as if calling in the coming night. A restrained Baroque church, trefoils and scrolls heavy around the doors, it would have been seen by Bach in its young prime. Musicians are gathering for evening practice. A feeling of melancholy longing comes over me. There are moments in some foreign journeys when the heart seems to lose its composure suddenly, to forget all reality and yearn to belong in some other where. I would not want to live in Wolfenbüttel, but some part of me wishes I were one of them, joining friends and collaborators for practice. Coming out of the gloaming, one by one, they disappear into the church. They will set out their instruments and settle themselves. They will tune up and gossip and come to order.

I love to watch these moments in concert halls, when you guess at the players' lives, and note their self-containment and the economy of their movements, and the frank way in which they put the audience aside as they lay out their music. And the sounds of their tuning up are bewitching, inexpressibly exciting, like the small jumbled cries of woodland birds which will, impossibly, sing as one. You are not spying on them because they know they are watched, but they act as though you are not there, so rather than voyeurism you practise a kind of visual eavesdropping as you watch them prepare, and guess at the words they exchange, and wonder who likes whom, and what they think of each other. Who has not momentarily longed to be one of them? Their disparate lives and instruments and parts assembling and sharing in creation, in the balance of art and science, harmony and melody.

Choristers, trombonists, violinists, viola players and oboists go into the church. They are rehearsing Bach's Cantata No. 2, *Ach Gott, vom Himmel sieh darein, Oh God, look down from heaven*. The words in the fantasia-like first chorus are from a hymn by Luther:

> O Lord, look down from heaven, behold
> And let Thy pity waken:
> How few are we within Thy Fold,
> Thy saints by men forsaken!
> True faith seems quenched on every hand,
> Men suffer not Thy Word to stand;
> Dark times have us o'ertaken...

Luther composed the hymn in Erfurt in 1524. Bach took it into his cantata in Leipzig and it was performed at the end of his first year there, in June 1724. Now it is to be performed here in Wolfenbüttel as part of the church's ongoing series of concerts. How ordinary and wonderful this seems at once – this ongoing way of life, this local production, this essence of this place, five centuries in the making and remade each night. It is inadequately described by 'culture'. Culture contains an implied limit, a border, a section of population and event, a period, a counterpoint in what is not culture. But this music in this church through all this time and onwards beyond foreseeable time seems to have no border. It was made here, is of here, in the same way the blackbirds' chinking and the darkening air are of here.

Luther drew on Psalm 12, a deep misery of a verse, written in a mode of depressive misanthropy (no one is faithful, everyone lies, the loyal have vanished, and so miserably on). Luther brightens it, and Bach further. The nihilism becomes melancholy, the despair becomes reflection, the tone is philosophical rather than misanthropic. Flights of hope never desert the soprano line.

As I write this, they are playing Cantata 51, *Praise God in Every Land*, at the Marienkirche. If you stopped the world at any moment, and measured all its live music in that instant, Beethoven and Mozart are likely to be the most played, with Bach third (there is an organisation which tracks classical performances). But then, as he might have pointed out, the other two followed Bach in time and craft.

We spend the night in Brunswick in a hotel of bizarre right angles and squares: ground plan, art, lifts, rooms, all are squares. At an Italian restaurant I am kidnapped by two friends, Gudrun and Steffi, who insist I go dancing with them.

'We have been extreme power shopping,' Gudrun says, as they consign bags of purchases to lockers. She is a powerful woman, gold-maned and blowsy, an instigator of action backed up by Steffi's darker, contingent and more jumpy presence.

'I want an open relationship but my husband does not want one and so Steffi has to lie for me,' Gudrun declares, airily. Steffi looks half-fraught, half-amused. They take me to the Flamingo Rosso, Brunswick's premier club, they say, which occupies the roof space of a steel and glass building. The dance floor is thronged, every torso swathed in a different perfume or aftershave. I think of a twisting enchanted wood, a jumping glade of scent, and I stay there until Gudrun and Steffi bid farewell. Bach surely had nights like these on his way, when he fell into company, and drank. Perhaps he danced.

The Road to Lüneburg

In Medingen, a village north of Brunswick, brick and timber buildings and chestnut trees drip with rain. Richard fiddles with batteries and waterproofing and a niggling noise on one of his microphones under the outer walls of Medingen's Abbey. A monastery which became a Lutheran women's convent in 1559, it was wealthy once, with access to trade from the Lüneburg saltworks, mills and boat traffic on the Ilmenau river.

'When I came through here on the recce there was a choir rehearsing *Jesu meine Freude,*' Lindsay says. 'Brought a tear to my eye I can tell you!'

Bach had lost three children, his first wife, Maria Barbara, and his brother Johann Jacob when he wrote the motet in Leipzig, possibly in 1723. The hymn's mood is beyond irony, in a space where grief and acceptance are cherished because they are at least not nothingness. It winds through dark and something else, a fragile illumination like candlelight, its breaths held in, subject to almost unholy control: it is full of measured feeling, mournful and disbelieving, its defiances are grave, its releases supplicatory, and its words by Johann Franck must have seemed to Bach idealistic in the extreme – *for those who love God their afflictions become sweetness.* Maybe not, but their music, now, their music just may... *Jesus my joy*, the closing phrase, is given with the most solemn, humble and resonant tone, the music working against the words, so that joy becomes a function of melancholy. There is terrible isolation in it, but the deep loneliness of soul at the end calls out softly with such tenderness that it is impossible, listening to it, not to feel there *is* a listener, that it is heard by its divine intended subject.

There is no question in this faith at all; there are questions – there are torments – in its progress and its demands, yes, but not in its conviction. How strange that Bach might have walked through this place with all this ahead of him. Three centuries later, the deaths of children he would have and a woman he was yet to wed would suffuse a piece of his which would reach beyond the walls he passed under and make a foreigner from the future cry. We seem to be venturing through nets of time so close together and far apart that they defy dimensions and our capacities to model them. In his fugues, Bach manipulates linear time so apparently effortlessly that it seems a plaything, an explanation given to a child on the understanding that at some future point the full mystery will make itself understood.

★

We are well north, fifteen to twenty days out of Arnstadt by the pacing of Bach's feet, and the roads and tracks are narrowing down towards Lüneburg. We are in or very near his footsteps again. The soil has altered, become sandy, and the trees have changed, too. Amid these fine, tall beechwoods Bach has become an adept and natural traveller, loose and fit, the events and adventures of the road rich and numerous between him and Arnstadt, which now feels far away. Dogs, eccentrics, beggars, beer, dancing and perhaps the company of one-night friends or lovers will have come together like a chrysalis, a collection of memories and experiences slightly out of time: he would never be so unwatched or unknown as he was on the road. With his only responsibility to himself, he could make or remake himself on his way as he wished.

You develop a kind of itinerant persona on a long walk, part pilgrim, part passage migrant, at home in your own space, which you bring into every village and hamlet. You sometimes see an extreme form on pilgrim trails, where a rangy figure in the midst of long conversation with him- or herself barely seems to see you, so intent is he or she upon the way, the road, the hostel.

When it rained like this, a light freshening rather than a soaking, he must have pulled his cloak on, set his hat and kept going, singing sometimes, or humming. It is easy to see him fuelling up and setting off into his days, the liberation of a stride out of town in the morning an equal counterpoint to the relief with which he tramped in at nightfall.

In soft November weather he walked through thick cushions of beech leaves, gold and bronze and red. There were jays then, too, the birds we see most often now. Jays are as exotic as rollers in their way, composites of all autumn's colours, catkin-pink chests, leaf-gold crowns, flashed with bright evening blue on their wings.

The path is marked with scallop shells; we have joined a pilgrim route, the Via Scandinavica, which has been incorporated into the E1 trail, a trans-Europe path running from Norway to Sicily, here running along a route which originally led from the Baltic to Rome. We pass no pilgrims, but Bach must have done; peculiarly independent figures, in communion with themselves as much as God, or perhaps with God in themselves, in their best moments. On the Camino Santiago in Spain, my partner Rebecca and I stayed in a pilgrim hostel which was haunted. I am not normally troubled by the other world, but there were many ghosts in this heavy-timbered place, a sense of spirits trapped in the walls and floorboards. Rebecca said she dreamed her feet were washed as she slept. There were no ghosts on Bach's daylight ways; they would have been shouldered aside on these paths, which must then have been thick with foot and horse-drawn traffic.

The great desertion of the countryside makes Europe's open spaces rather sad in their silences. This is a leisured landscape; it's like a forgotten toy, the stumpy watchtowers of the hunting fraternity like abandoned tree-houses. Although hoof-prints show that riders have been here, there is no other sign of people among the small pasture fields, which are tended – at least their fences are – but unused. This northern edge of Lower Saxony, intricate and melancholy in the rain, is much more beautiful than the southern country's huge agricultural heaves.

We cross the Ilmenau, a sweet river, two canals wide and flowing northwards through water meadows. There are deer at the wood's edge and the light is more northerly, whiter somehow, falling on pines and beech. The way is fine walking. Just as their Audis and Mercedes eat the autobahns, so the German walker has the fastest routes in Europe underfoot. You can make distance here unimpeded by contours, bogs or rough ground, I find myself thinking, and suddenly we lose our way, a bog, a hedge line and a tangle of thickets conspiring to beguile us.

I get a fit of the giggles as the rain thickens and Richard struggles to make condoms stay on his microphones.

'Unlubricated,' he intones, 'You used to be able to get them from the production stores but now you have to order them from a website.'

'We're here,' Lindsay says, flapping his map. 'Here somewhere.'

'You're so lost!'

Bach stands and watches us, hand on hip, slightly smiling. He has been composing this morning; he has notes in his pocket and he has thought of another line of questions for the old radical, Buxtehude. Some things about our art... These odd pursuers, he thinks, with their memorising machines, their maps, their muttering.

He would have been good with the media, Johann Sebastian, seeing us as allies and accelerators, a way around the stifles of preferment, advancement, patronage, a way to reach thousands over hundreds, millions over thousands.

*

I have been listening to his keyboard duets, BWV 802 to 805. The lilting, dancing statements seem all questions, reminiscent of children twirling: can you do this? And this? Watch this! The answers are full of flight and caprice, as though a second dancer has heard the questions but asks them again, half-answers, makes comments and never quite leaves the dance of the first without ever quite joining it. Again and again he resolves propositions by expanding upon them, the way beauty expands beyond its beginnings, nature beyond her seeds. His joy is so intense that his mourning is almost unbearable.

Bach in a wood in the rain... I do not believe he was ever caught out by weather. Thorough preparation is part of who he is, the orphan boy, the nation of one; you can see him thinking in pieces like the duets as he pushes on under a light rain which vivifies rather than depresses a solitary walker. The duets are lines of lyric poetry, as if written to be played in solitude, heard in solitude, as if near-empty rooms surround them. I see flowers in vases in sunlight.

We tramp through the woods, arrested by the sight of bracket fungi on a beech stump, a glowing alien saucer-city, black with glowing white edges. A fugue of them climb the stump like lines of notes on a score. The woods stand taller and thinner, younger trees flitting and clicking in the rain. The moisture and the clouds soak light out of the sky, but our morale is excellent. Lindsay refolds his maps; Richard is thinking about a rabbit: his girlfriend is threatening to get one while he is away. We rest at a fence line, changing wet socks for dry, and push on into open country.

Now the bridges over the Ilmenau are guarded by signs

in black and yellow: tanks are not to exceed 50 kilometres an hour. The remnants of the British Army on the Rhine are based to the west, in Nort Rhine-Westphalia, but the sense of a landscape plotted over, prepared and measured for a war which has not come still lingers.

The quietly majestic scale of Germany seems to speak of old power and new potential, something expanding and expansive. The houses, gardens and villages, even the individual rooms, of Germany are all bigger than their British equivalents. There is just more space here, and a feeling of freedom in it. No wonder so many of the writers, scholars and technical innovators of my generation are or have been based in Berlin. Whenever I have visited they have spoken of freedom, of space, of not being overlooked and monitored as the British are, of being able to afford to live cheaply and think in ways they could not in London, of a life less constrained than Britain offers. I attended a dinner party there, taken cross-legged on the floor of a large flat with few furnishings, where there were eight nationalities, half a dozen vocations, at least three languages in general use, and a feeling of easy and wonderful possibility. When I asked for the secret of Berlin, a mature student said, 'It's the space. You go that way, east, and there's a thousand kilometres of the same landscape all the way from here through Poland to Lithuania. And Berlin is the centre of it all, in a way – so much space.'

Lindsay and Richard are more patriotic than me. When I ask them for marks, they both give Germany 'seven out of ten.'

★

At the little village of Bruchtorf, horses run; a dark mare and a grey flying through their paddock, their manes wild, their energy and companionship ecstatic. Richard captures the thrumming charge of their hoofbeats on the microphone and Lindsay thanks them, delighted. The light now belongs neither to afternoon nor to evening as the sky begins to shoal and break, the sun casting a silvery light from the west. A pure clear line forms to the north, dim turquoise, and there are soft bars like gills above us. I hope he came along here. He would have been a deeply happy young man on an evening like this, all his tension and the anger of Arnstadt walked into the ground. Other walkers, students and travelling musicians must have passed him. Itinerant musicians were the stars of a sub-genre of popular novels at the time, rakes and seducers, impecunious and artistic, ideal vehicles for their writers, some of whom were musicians themselves, to tell tales of adventure, liaison and mischief. I bet he had musical conversations, at his night stops if not on the road. I bet he made the short friendships of minutes or hours which lighten a moment, an evening, a day.

The country is lovely now: rides and hangers and stands of beech trees, and ploughed fields running to rich woodland like a Samuel Palmer painting. A lady with two dachshunds approaches, one a puppy misbehaving as she scolds it lovingly, charm itself. Brown slugs scatter the path as the smell of birches and oaks surround us, that damp sweetness of evening and the rising dew. The scents of autumn are rich and strong, field and hedge and woodland all different and intermingled. He walked through an aromatic landscape, the air much clearer then than it is now, its odours stronger, human population and pollution being fractions of what they are now.

We watch the sky as it dims and I think he must have become adept at reading the weather patterns; when you can see the sky here you can generally see a lot of it. I wonder how much he walked at night. On fairly busy roads, with a good moon, you could easily keep going. The sun goes down leaving crimson scripts and a huge flourish of flared cloud above pine forestry. There is a touch of the Gothic, a spirit-shiver in the coming night. Did he ever feel very lonely on his walk? There must have been moments of great loneliness in his young life, times of isolation; perhaps he was ever, as I imagine Shakespeare was, something of a man apart. Travel on foot or otherwise is good for that, though. With your mind on the road and the achievement of the thing, you have less time to dwell. Isolation in stasis is much worse. In some of his music you can hear the time of composition, the night silence around him, the candle guttering and the pen crossing the pages.

We reach Wichmannsburg, a small clutch of houses with their eyes closed, as peaceful and nondescript a place as exists anywhere, and the light fails as two cats assess two horses in a field. We push on to Bienenbüttel where we take a train back to Bad Bevensen and the car. Lindsay and I contract appalling fits of giggles on the train, as the machine won't sell us a ticket, and Lindsay's crime wave (he was flashed by a speed camera yesterday) continues. Breaking the law in other countries does not feel entirely illegal, we agree. Richard and I calculate he is on several crimes a day, although I am unsure how we arrive at this figure.

Less fit than Bach, we are weary now, but still, the short drive to Lüneburg is a thumping transposition of our time onto his. The last sections of the day are incomparably lovely walking: you want a tiny hotel, now, and no choice on the menu – whatever they have and a glass of beer – and the torpid slumber of the countryside and the listening silence of woods beyond the windows. Instead, we follow motorway and satnav to a swishy hotel in Lüneburg, where we duck in from a cold night, eat Italian food and take early to our beds. You close your eyes to places when you arrive tired: you perceive as a child perceives, in flashes, impressions, like dream fragments. Lüneburg is the dark water of the Ilmenau and a cold intimating frost, and medieval buildings along the river, overhanging, leaning on each other, their faces like aged aristocrats grown warty and magisterial.

The Old Salt Road

It is supposed to have begun with a white wild boar, shot by a hunter, her bristles encrusted with crystals. Not snow, but salt: the boar had been rolling in a saline spring which betrayed the presence of a salt dome in the ground beneath Lüneburg. By the time of Bach's residence here, as a chorister at the Michaeliskirche in 1700, the salt trade was past its Hanseatic peak, but it had built a rich and cultured city with strong traditions of music and patronage. Lüneburg salt, shipped up the River Ilmenau or carted up the Salt Road to Lübeck and the coast, had been worth almost as much as gold in the late twelfth century. The herring-rich diet of the Baltic region meant a market which stretched all the way to Norway and Sweden. So much salt was mined from under the city that in one quarter its buildings began to subside: a number of them, and a church, had to be knocked down. Many of the older structures still lean. Despite a decline in profits in the late sixteenth century, salt was still mined here until 1980.

Bach would have seen much of the trade, its merchants, tycoons and legacies.

Before his voice broke Bach sang treble in the Michaeliskirche choir; we do not know what part he sang after the week of its breaking – during which he could only speak in octaves – probably falsetto with the trebles, or with the sopranos. But his scholarship and singing were successful: he was afforded free board and lodging, a small wage and instruction in the St Michaelis church school, which was outstanding, prestigious and built on four centuries of education when Bach enrolled.

His curriculum included rhetoric, Latin, Greek and German verse. The Bach scholar Peter Williams points out that the library at the Michaeliskirche was then one of the best-stocked in Protestant Germany: Bach's decision to make for Lüneburg, whether made by himself or, more likely, in collusion with his brother Christoph, bore rich fruit. Perhaps crucially for an orphan, he also had the company of at least one friend to whom he would remain close for many years, Georg Erdmann, with whom he made the journey here from Ohrdruf. Bach flourished, a scholar at the top of his class. His son Emanuel's obituary records Bach being 'well-received' in the town, a tribute indeed to a fifteen-year-old boy. He had fun here, too. The choirs of St Michaelis and St Johannis were furious rivals. Busking in Lüneburg's cobbled streets was lucrative and highly competitive. The best pitches were physically fought over. For a boy with Bach's attitude to authority and sense of self-possession it must have been a rich time: independent in the world, making his own way, successful at school and in his work of singing, befriended, busy and with opportunities for letting off steam with rowdy and abrasive competition, which he must have relished.

Our morning breaks bright-blue over the hard red tiles of the old town. The brick-and-timber-framed buildings, crow-step roofs, the flights of doves and pigeons and the frontage, like galleons reflected in the river, Bach would have seen and known well. A statue of Mark Twain reclines on a bench by the river: debts, ill-health and a block in the middle of *Adventures of Huckleberry Finn* drove him here with his wife and daughter in 1878. He loved Germany, wrote a travel book (*A Tramp Abroad*) and found a balance with which he returned to America, the novel and the greatest decade of his career. It is rather delightful to bump into another foreign writer abroad, like walking across the bridge in Trieste and finding yourself face to face with Joyce.

Passing through Lüneburg must have been exciting. (No, there is no documentary evidence he stopped here on his walk, but you would have to detour around it, extravagantly and deliberately, in order *not* to come here on a journey from Arnstadt to Lübeck. It bestrides the route – and the Salt Road was part footpath, part highway leading straight to his goal. He came here, alright.) The nostalgia of the young for the recent past can be overwhelming; to return to a place where you were happy three years ago, at twenty, is like looking over a small chasm into the end of childhood and the budding of youth. How young you were then! Standing outside his church, St Michaelis, a towering brick Gothic sibling to the Marienkirche in Lübeck, where he was bound, we speculate about his time here.

'I bet he met a woman,' Lindsay says.

'For sure! I hope he came back to see her,' I return.

'Hope he treated her well.'

'A good egg, that Bach,' I tease him.

'Or maybe he steered clear.'

'Something had happened and he couldn't come back. She was heartbroken!'

'Or he went out with his mates and never looked her up,' says Lindsay.

'Hmm. Bit mean.'

'Well, he was only young.'

Lindsay has a deep love and knowledge of Bach's music. He has come to him here along a much more learned and respectful path than mine. (It takes this journey and this journal for me to begin to comprehend the scale of Bach's genius.) And yet, compared to Shakespeare, alive only a century before Bach and my nearest point of comparison with him, we know a huge amount about him. We can hear Shakespeare's inner being only in whispers and tones, as asides in the hubbub of his characters' voices and in his poems' personae, while we can hear Bach's feelings in every note. Perhaps words conceal you in some way that music does not. Yet Lindsay and I both feel that we are closing in on a figure behind it all, this young man, full of appetite and energy.

Did he work too hard to follow a young man's pursuits? Possibly. A chorister's day started early and let up but little. In his free time he made journeys from Lüneburg to Hamburg to hear the famous organist of St Catherine's, Johann Adam Reincken. He may have been urged to these expeditions by a tutor and mentor, Georg Böhm. Böhm was the organist at St Johannis, the rival church, but their friendship grew across the divide:

they were in contact for years afterwards: in 1727, Bach would name the older man as the agent for the sale of six harpsichord suites, the first of his compositions to be commercially published. Emanuel records that his father 'loved and studied Böhm's work'. Böhm is judged 'the most gifted composer Sebastian could have come across so far,' by Bach's biographer Peter Williams. Böhm knew Hamburg's ebullient musical life, both its theatre and church music, and may have encouraged Bach's trips. Emanuel's obituary states that from Lüneburg Bach also went to Celle, where he had the chance 'through frequent listening to a then famous band kept by the Duke of Celle, and consisting largely of Frenchmen, to give himself a good grounding in French taste, which at the time was something entirely new in those parts.'

Another biographer, Christoph Wolff, is in no doubt as to Böhm's influence. Böhm introduced Bach, Wolff writes, 'to the genre of stylised dance in general, and to French music and performance practices in particular … he also provided Bach with compositional models – preludes and fugues of his own and of other Northern composers as well as chorale variations, a genre in which he excelled.'

Partly from Lüneburg, then, comes the 'dance-impregnated' quality of Bach's music and person identified by John Eliot Gardiner, though its seeds must have been planted in infancy, listening to his father's piping. Gardiner believes it is likely that Bach lodged with Böhm, though the evidence is ambiguous, the abbreviated Latin word 'Dom' in Bach's hand on a manuscript either referring to Böhm as his master, or to his house as the place of composition.

The young Bach at St Michaeliskirche was clearly a teenager of deep seriousness with regard to his art and craft, but one wonders if listening to and making music was a sufficient outlet for the steam of adolescence. We know his workload in later life was staggering: there can never have been a time, from a very young age, when he was not engaged in his art. Given his accomplishments and his extremely long hours, it is difficult not to think of his walk as one of the few moments in his career when he was away from his desk for much time. And because we are on the road, his road, it is hard not to sense a side to him that drank and flirted and argued, hungry for more than food. He liked sex and beer, it is certain – he would father twenty children – and he was surely possessed of a relishing personality.

The interior of his first great church is a reverie of terracotta pink on entering, which resolves into blushing fine brickwork as you focus. The Michaeliskirche lost its medieval furnishings during an overhaul at the end of the eighteenth century, but the brick, the colours, the height and scale are as they were, and must have been dazzling even to a boy accustomed to such lofty and sacred spaces.

The organ, much restored, descends from an original which was installed in 1708. The machine Bach knew and played occupied the same space on a similar scale. The spare Protestant interior affords little prominence to anything but the light, the altar, a few pictures and the organ, and of these the organ is the most magnificent. It was not always so. Bach just missed seeing the Golden Panel, the Goldene Tafel, a Romanesque antependium and masterpiece of golden metalwork hanging from the front of the altar. Two years before he arrived it was stolen and melted down by robbers (only the wings survive in the Museum August Kestner in Hanover). In its absence, the organ seems to be more than half the point of the church. Although placed behind the congregation, it still overshadows the altar.

There is a happiness attending the story of his years here. Georg Böhm must have been responsible for part of it. Bach's first biographer, Johann Nikolaus Forkel, writing fifty years after Bach's death, says that Bach's teaching encouraged his pupils to take risks. 'He let them dare whatever they would and could.... As he himself attempted everything possible in this respect, he liked to see his scholars do the same.' We do not know Böhm's teaching methods, but star pupils often adopt the practices of their best instructors, and so it seems likely Böhm encouraged Bach to experiment, to learn and grow in every direction that drew him. Bach must have known the church as pupils know a classroom. What an exalting ship it must have made for his thoughts and hopes and daydreams, as it seared itself into the young chorister's mind's eye and memory. Of all his unimaginable, uncountable legacy, the knowledge of the church's future address would surely have given him a gleeful pleasure: St Michaeliskirche, Johann-Sebastian-Bach Platz, 21335 Lüneburg.

We cross the mighty Elbe, deep blue and too big to be called busy, but bearing a few barges and converted fishing vessels, all the same. On a glittering day, minted in heaven and sent down for the pleasure of the people of western Europe, we walk into high autumn, one of those singing mornings that intimate the coming of bright winter. Horses stand dreamily in the cool air, letting the sun warm their coats, while fifty mute swans, like fat white slugs, pick over a field of deep green. We walk through mixed woodland, larch, pine, hazel and birch and beech. The smell of the larches in the clear air is as sharp and pointed as their needles, the scents of the track a sweet intermingling of pine and larch and earth and dew. A buzzard cries above us, the true call of the gentle wild, that longing, summoning keen. You rarely seem them in savage nature: the buzzard is a bird of the in-betweens, where wood meets field, where pasture becomes hill. They are more for slopes than the high mountains. There are too many ravens up there, which give buzzards trouble. Something in the air has put the birds in gay spirits. A red kite floats over us next, easily turning under the mobbings of a carrion crow. The crow keeps coming around and flapping in and trying again, and the kite disdains it, tiny adjustments to her wings and russet tail slipping her out of reach, her timing sublime, a maestro against a *zippel Fagottist*.

Bach sets out with us, much refreshed from his Lüneburg stay. No doubt he had seen Georg Böhm and apprised him of his plans. If Eliot Gardiner is right, and Bach had lodged with Böhm before, then perhaps he did so again. Scholars have detected Böhm's influence in a clutch of Bach's works, particularly in the early chorale partitas BWV 766–70, probably composed in Lüneburg under Böhm's tutelage. The first, *Christ, der du bist der helle Tag*

(*Christ, you are the light of day*) is doubly apposite this morning. It has a delightfully exploratory quality, the organ striding forth, puffed up with the confidence of starting out, a stately chorale indeed, which then quietens and complicates, simple harmonies dividing into two-part variations as it strolls on. No great consequence or feeling attends the piece, but it is more than a technical exercise. It feels young, though not juvenile; there is a recognition of beauty's transience in its lighter passages, and the seventh variation stretches upwards and deepens, closing with a resonance and solemnity which feel slightly put-on, but restrainedly, respectfully so. You can almost see him lifting his hands from the keys and looking up for Böhm's reaction. If music does reveal some deep part of us which words do not (compare a writer's prose and poetry: how much more exposing is the more musical form), then the chorale partitas summon a dedicated, brave young writer, brave enough to allow himself to be vulnerable, his music working between something delicate and careful and something much more longing. He is tangibly still on the leash, but learning, learning all the time.

He is just under 60 miles from Lübeck now, three or four days' travel, the weather peerless if it was like this, the joy of the road in his feet. He must have felt invincible as he regained his walking rhythm. We are all bouncy this morning, laughing and high-spirited as we cross in and out of blazes of sun which lie in bright slashes through the shade of spruce and pines. Being as certain as scholars can be that we are in his footsteps again has lifted us since Lüneburg. Schleswig-Holstein's landscape here is small agricultural fields and mature, tall woodland, astonishing pines above us with splashes of gold-green light on their trunks, and in the lower canopy, oak. It is a morning for seeing deer or unicorns, we decide. The leaves fall in very slow journeys to the ground, as if making the most of their flight.

In glades of Scots pine I look for honey buzzards and goshawks. A Scots pine is the scene of the action in my most treasured memory of childhood reading, in BB's *Brendon Chase*, where Robin makes a terrifying climb to a honey buzzard's nest. He retrieves an egg, the birds mewing pitifully around him, but all is well – the egg is addled, and Robin has his treasure. Honey buzzards do nest in Germany: they breed successfully here, but they are summer migrants, overwintering now in sub-Saharan Africa. There are common buzzards in the distant blue. A green woodpecker like a small flying dragon dips towards us down the track. We cross a bridge over a loud autobahn and a female sparrowhawk flushes from right to left in front of us, a serpentine ferocity in her wild eye. The sandy soil and pebbles underfoot and the gentle undulations of the land towards the coast suggest that we are walking through the memories of ancient sea beds, where the coastline has retreated.

I look for oak trees he would have passed by. Counting the rings on piles of Scots pine logs gives thirty to forty years for these young trees, but an oak takes three hundred years to grow, three hundred years to live and three hundred to die... There! There is a grove of the sturdy trees, standing like councillors in conversation. They were saplings when young Johann Sebastian came nipping by. When he came up here the Salt Road was already old.

In 1398, one of the earliest artificial waterways in Europe was completed, the Stecknitz canal, linking Lauenburg, 14 miles north of Lüneburg, to Lübeck, which meant the bulk of cargoes went by boat. But wagons continued to carry it up the Salt Road, which was much safer in Bach's time than it had been. At the height of the trade, in the sixteenth century, with over 19,000 tons of the crystals being transported between the two cities, the road was imperilled by robbers and thieves. It runs between humped tumps covered in beech trees (perfect cover for a desperado's ambush) and meadows; it is direct, wide and north-driving, but in rain and under heavy use it would bog and slough. Bach must have picked his way between the ruts and horse dung.

Parts of the track were cobbled and have been resurfaced in the same way; the roll of the pale blue and pink flint blocks under the balls of your feet makes it easy to imagine the noise carts and horse-shoes would have made over them. There was less peace for composition and sustained thought here than he would have had back in the woods. The presence of business and merchant traffic would have bolstered his resolve and quickened his pace, perhaps. He was no idle stroller, as the set of his shoulders and his pace must have conveyed to any who noticed. A young artist approaching a big city might have done some self-reinforcement. I am Johann Sebastian Bach. I have business (even though he does not know it yet) with Dieterich Buxtehude in the Marienkirche. But steadily on, steadily on. There are a couple of days to go yet. At least he was sure of accommodation. Every village along this track must have had facilities and traditions of hospitality that went back centuries. Now the Salt Road turns eastwards towards the Elbe-Lübeck canal, known as the Stecknitz canal in Bach's day, one of the earliest artificial waterways in Europe.

'Do you want to tell us about you and Bach then, H?' Lindsay asks.

'Sure,' I say, jauntily, but I do not feel jaunty about it. In 1753, three years after Bach's death, his son Emanuel published an essay on how to play keyboard instruments. We may be sure, as his father's pupil, that the points Emanuel makes were made to him by his father.

'In languishing sad passages the performer must languish and grow sad. Thus will the expression of the piece be more clearly perceived by the audience... Similarly, in lively, joyous passages, the executant must again put himself into the appropriate mood. And so, constantly varying the passions, he will barely quiet one before be rouses another.'

In the same way, you cannot properly relate the story of a hard time without in part reliving its difficulty, and my personal relationship with Bach goes back to such a time. Through my childhood my knowledge of classical music was almost entirely church-based; I knew many hymns and carols, I had sung a great deal through school – with enthusiasm, if not talent – and I had heard but not much engaged with pieces by Elgar, Vivaldi, Holst and Mozart; the rest was pop, rock, hip hop, trip hop and indie until I reached university. There, my girlfriend, a cellist, introduced me to Chopin, Schubert, Debussy and some Bach, but by the time we broke up in our third year my collection of tapes and compact discs contained only four classical records, all given to me by my father: Schubert and Chopin (both piano sonatas) Mozart (violin concertos) and Bach's cello suites.

The break-up was part of it, but I think it was more symptom than cause of my first encounter with depression. The awful thing was that I did not know what was happening to me. The vocabulary of mental health was less common and narrower then: in three years at university I never once heard the term 'anxiety' used as it is now, for example. Some kind of collapse into terror and hopelessness seemed to come over me, almost overnight. I had a small room looking out over rooftops and I could barely leave it. Finals were approaching, there was a great deal of work and no option of not doing it, and so I sat at my desk and tried and tried to write the notes and essays. I ground the words out one at a time.

Outside, spring was burgeoning towards summer, and the world's colours and lights were rejoicing, while in the room I felt a ceaseless, crushing beat of self-loathing and despair. An insistent part of me wanted to die. The piles of pop and rock, even the best of it – Bowie, Dylan, Joni Mitchell – seemed to have nothing to do with me anymore. I was in a place unreachable by any of them until I put the cello suites into the CD player.

There are words for depression, there are words about depression, but depression despises words. Depression eats words and steals them, returns them in truncated, frightened clumps. It narrows words into closed loops; depression chants and scours across all of existence, reducing it to tight constricting words, harrowing those words down to refrains, stunting their generative power, stunning the faculties which produce them – a mist, a fog, a tumult of depression: words will supply metaphors without end, but they hang, greyly listless, as pointless as everything else, to the depressed. There is one main refuge from depression, when you are in it, which is unconsciousness, and there, too, words follow you, may even comfort you in dreams, though they leave you inadequate, misled and desperate when you wake.

Perhaps that is why the cello suites were so kind to me then: because there is not a word anywhere near them, because they construct, inhabit and invite you to a place beyond them. It is a place of safety, soft and intimate and quietly, insistently uplifting. There is an odd calm in the music, the calm of slow delight. Two forces seem to combine through the pieces, two atmospheres of time – the present, in which the notes run, and somewhere else: a thing, a place, a braid of feeling and understanding, inexpressible and never directly addressed, which may be God, or life in death, or a peace of which the mind is not consciously capable, but which exists, still and forever.

I did not say this when Lindsay asked me to speak about the cello suites. Instead, I explained that I had grown up with books on a farm, and that all my relationships were with writers and, later, painters and sculptors.

Walking along, which is the best way to be when talking about painful things, my feet on the flint cobbles of the Old Salt Road, I told the story.

'It wasn't until university and my third year and my first encounter with real, naked, vicious depression that I started listening to the cello suites, and I listened to them again and again and again, with that intensity that somebody deeply ignorant of the whole field of classical music could listen to a thing which – to me, anyway – was all classical music. And it is emotional to even think about it, because the depth and the emotion and the suggestion of the music was profound, and in depression you feel very intensely what you feel, and one of the better things about life then was that CD. And so were I to meet Bach, my questions would all obviously – as one writer who travels to another – be about this journey, and about his return journey, and his adventures, and how close were we in our suppositions? And did we get it right? And where did he stop? And did he go over the Harz mountains? But then I'd have to say to him, in the way that you sometimes do – my literary life has occasionally brought me into contact with my heroes and heroines, and you have to be a bit careful, but you can't help sounding like the super fan that you are. So I remember telling Seamus Heaney that I thought he was wonderful, and just thanking him for *being* – and I think I would have to say something to Johann Sebastian about those cello suites and how they really helped get me through a very hard time. They gave beauty and truth and hope in a period when there seemed very little. So I think... I'd have lots of questions, and just a couple of statements.'

It is a special day, the walk on the Old Salt Road. At lunch, halfway between the woods and the canal, we lie down on a dead-end road at the edge of a wide field and eat sausages and bread and take off our shoes, our equipment strewn about us, and we relax in the sun. I have coaxed quite a lot out of Richard by this time. He had a choice between being a pop star with a group he would probably prefer I did not name and being a studio manager with the BBC. He chose the BBC, sensible man. Sometimes, though, he accepts a plane ticket and flies to another country or another continent to guest as a pianist or drummer. I find he is one of those people whom I delight to make laugh, so we continue teasing Lindsay about his 'crime sprees'.

'Tell me some studio manager secrets, Richer Sounds.'

'We have the DFA fader.'

'What's that?'

'The Does Fuck-All fader. If someone's hanging around pissing you off, asking for changes in the sound, you reach out and move the DFA fader. Or pretend to move it. And then they leave you alone.'

'What else?'

'You never fade the Queen.'

'Ha! Really?'

'It's the first rule. Never Fade the Queen. Whatever she says, she can go on for as long as she likes, you don't fade her down.'

'Right. Good to know...'

I try to draw him on the BBC technical training centre in the grounds of a stately home near Evesham, where studio managers are instructed in the arts of keeping the nation going – or at least able to hear something intelligible coming out of the radio – in the event of Armageddon, but he heads me off with citrus fruit.

'And there's the lemons.'

'What lemons?'

'It's a joke that got out of hand. Someone left a lemon in an OB truck. And then someone hid some in the flight cases with the equipment. Now whenever you get an OB truck there will be lemons in the cases. It got to the point where people were hiding melons.'

We switch to Lindsay again.

'You know what they say about classical music producers and outside broadcasts,' Richard says.

'Recidivists? Crooks?'

'Yeah. You set up the whole OB – Glyndebourne or the Proms or whatever – and then finally the producer turns up to 'balance the orchestra'. Which basically means he gets them to play something, listens to the output, nods, and goes out to lunch with the talent.'

'That sounds about right. What's the Proms like?'

'Loads of work, obviously, but you have to stop yourself sometimes. Like, I'm knackered, my break's way overdue, I've got loads on – but it is actually just me in the whole Albert Hall with Daniel Barenboim down there rehearsing the Staatskapelle Berlin.'

We walk on into the afternoon, the cello suites in my thoughts. Their slow beauty is like the mind thinking at first, then going beyond thinking into that gently entwined place where feeling, memory and daydream interweave. They summon glimpses of your past and fragments of visions untethered from the more or less linear narrative of life. Here you are at seven, opening a gate with your parents, and now at twenty-seven, making supper with your lover, and now at fourteen, on a Sunday in a church, and now at an unknown age, by the sea in summer. They seem at a certain and miraculous distance from existence; so unhurried that they somehow move the listener to a place a little way back, where all things seem equal before the music. It is the opposite of the impression of life flashing before your eyes, reported by people in moments of dire crisis: instead, the suites seem, gravely and slowly, to measure out a scale that extends the dimensions which life usually accords and within which it is normally lived. You listen to them with a sense of recognition for unexpressed beauties and sadnesses, as though you are brought by the notes to see and hear those currents which flow through you always – in barely perceptible drifts, mostly, but in roaring torrent sometimes – and which comprise your deeper self. The music seems to expose the angle at which you truly stand in relation to the world, somewhere far above or outside the petty regimentations and stresses of status and situation. Though they are not explicitly religious pieces, the suites have a power and a humility which takes the listener to the same place that the religious describe when they talk of the mysteries of faith, of states of grace and divine comfort. The music seems by turns wise and melancholy, ruefully amused sometimes, and philosophical, both accepting and longing. It is as though a sky cannot be quite large enough to contain the gentle venerations of the cello, as though horizons will not quite hold them. Something like a breeze moves the listener, a breeze both invisible and tangible, like the white space between the black printed words of a poem, where all the truth and certainty lie, in convictions which we hold and know but can never fully express.

★

Rowers skim past in skiffs, and a kingfisher shoots a dart of raw blue dazzle low along the bank. There are black-headed gulls and ducks, enough life for the eye, but we are in that part of a walk before the end, when anticipation trumps the present moment and you rather wish you could go faster. Evening finds us in the suburbs of Mölln, where we taxi back to where we left the car. We drive to Lübeck, arriving in the dark. After all our anticipation, it feels like entering a kind of holy city.

Lübeck

A free imperial city from 1226 to 1937 (which meant its council answered to the Holy Roman Emperor in Vienna, rather than any local duke), Lübeck, then as now, is a rich and thrilling destination, a spired city on a low hill looped by the Trave river. We stroll up into the town in search of dinner and find the Schiffergesellschaft, a truly splendid sixteenth-century eating hall of long banqueting tables (if Bach came here he would have rested his elbows on the same wood), benches and partitions, hung with paintings and dozens of model ships. From 1535, this was a meeting place of sea captains, brokers and shipping agents: they were assigned tables according to their ports and corporations. Something of their confidence and thrust remains in the faces around us, Hanseatic faces, I think, long and well-fed, wealthy and observant. We feast on chops and steaks, and order tall clay pots of beer. The power of the Hanseatic League had declined by the time Bach made his entry here in 1705, but this was still a cosmopolitan and teeming city, crow-stepped houses tall and elegant along the waterfronts. Cobbled streets run between them up to the churches. Lübeck stands at the junction where the network of inland waterways meets the rivers to the sea. Lüneburg salt and all the spices, silks, tobaccos, wines, fish, metals, skins, furs, cloth, grain and trade goods of the world passed through it, the imports and exports of the Holy Roman Empire crossing in its warehouses and on its quays. You would have been fortunate to be born here, and happy to work here, in a town on a human scale with national and international reach.

At daybreak, residents are jogging along the river past the concert hall and Lübeck retains a haughty, glittering self-possession on this last morning of our expedition, mist rising from the waters into bright air and the spires of the Marienkirche adrift in pearlescent low cloud, which blends sky and sun in a gay and vaporous intermingling.

We start at the city's western gateway, the Holstentor, built in 1478, a massy fortress of brick and conical towers. As any traveller, Bach would have felt jubilation and significance as he passed through the arched tunnel of its entrance. In 1705, it would have been the third of four he walked through in a row, the last on the far other side of the Trave river: a sense of destination, arrival and delight would have been boosted by each one. We are all excited. By long walking, following, mulling and researching we have put ourselves in the way of Bach, close on the heels of his ghost, almost by his side. We are hoping for serendipity now, for some unpredictable connection. Radio, like writing and walking, needs luck. You can do much to put yourself in its path, but in the end success is also a matter of chance, or synchronicity, or karma. I do not know what is going to happen but I feel something, close and electrifying, this beautiful and exalting morning.

We pass through the gate and over the river, the cool green smell of the water rising. Long before industrialisation and the motorcar a town like this must have been a feast of the scents of baking, horses, fish, tar and cooking fires. The spires of the Marienkirche, Saint Mary's, rise and beckon us, their tops tangled in mist. If Bach arrived in daylight he must have headed straight for them. Gulls squeal around moored sailing barges as we cross into the city and climb the cobbled streets. Four more spires appear in the mist and Bach's mind now must have been a whirl; he must have thought his way across his whole short life on his walk, and now he is nearly there and Buxtehude so close. How will the old man receive him? What will Bach say to him?

The church is huge above you as you approach up the gentle hill; it stands on the highest point of old Lübeck's island. At over 400 feet high, the twin brick Gothic spires spear the sky, their points sheathed in green copper. Along each flank ranks of flying buttresses martial the tremendous down-force of the towers and the vaulted nave, the tallest brick-built vault in the world, at 120 feet. What a holy citadel has Buxtehude in which to make his music, Bach thinks. He rounds the side of the church and enters the Medieval courtyard, passing a block of granite, which legend has it was left there by the devil, who had been tricked into helping with the construction of the building in the thirteenth century, on the understanding it would be a wine bar. He was dissuaded from destroying the church by a promise that a bar would be built nearby, which it was, but he returned on the moonlit night of March 28, 1942, when the Royal Air Force dropped over 500 tonnes of bombs, their first attack on a civilian population, designed to create a firestorm and spread terror and despair. The church was rebuilt after the War; the door I push open is a reconstruction of the one Bach came through, but the space we enter is exactly the same.

Three deep breaths, and Johann Sebastian seems right beside me now as I go in. He turns the handle, enters and looks up. There is an electric feeling of his presence now: he takes off his hat; we both do. The church is up-soaring inside, built on the same principles as French cathedrals of the time, and my spine seems to tingle as I enter the nave, high and mighty, the walls red and green, the ceiling decorated with birds and flowers. There is no doubt in me as to what Bach did now. It happens as if automatically: his hat off, he gazed up and he sat on a pew, full of a prayerful feeling of gratitude and fulfilment. Done it. Now he listens to the space, to the acoustic, and he feels both small and uplifted as you do in a place like the Marienkirche: diminutive but special, too, because God's architects promise that all are special in His sight, and because Johann Sebastian was special, and there for his particular purpose, for something of his art.

And then, because he was so directed, he looked around, studied the organ high on the back wall (the 'danse macabre' organ, the one Buxtehude played, and which Bach may have tried, was destroyed in the air raid) and wondered where he might find the man he had come to see. He noted the balconies and minstrel galleries that Buxtehude was able to fill with musicians, giving his concerts a wide stereophony. I rise and circle around the nave to the western end, beneath the towers and the organ, and there on the wall is a plaque, a simple sculpture showing an elderly, bewigged man seated at an organ, and behind him a young and nervous figure holding a sheaf of music. It is only a symbolic representation, bearing no resemblance, but it is rather wonderful to find him here, in this second depiction of him, marking the end of his journey from Arnstadt. I feel very proud of him, for his defiance, his self-determination, his perseverance and the triumph of his arrival.

He had only taken four weeks' leave, but a stay of three months suggests things went well for him in Lübeck. Though we do not know where he lodged or who he met, we can be sure he was here in the Marienkirche for Buxtehude's evening concerts of *Abendmusik* on the second, third and fourth Sundays of Advent, and for performances of music composed to mark the death of the Emperor Leopold I and the accession of Joseph I in December 1705. Of two cantatas Buxtehude is known to have performed in December 1705, one, BuxWV 135, had a 25-piece string section, the largest company Bach would have heard so far. Bach's must have become a familiar face in the Marienkirche. It is inconceivable that he did not become acquainted with Buxtehude. If there was an opening in the company of musicians or any opportunity to play for Buxtehude, Bach surely took it: he would have seized any chance, and perhaps he was able to earn a fee. It is overwhelmingly likely that the older man did let him copy his manuscripts: Buxtehude's Praeludium in C major, BuxWV137, has survived in the so-called 'Andreas Bach Book', a collection copied out by Bach's brother Christoph. The score for the Praeludium surely came back to Thuringia in his younger brother's knapsack. As far as we know he undertook the return journey in February 1706, also on foot, and certainly through hard winter weather. We have been following a very robust and dauntless young man.

For all the wealth of influence and ideas that he gathered in the Marienkirche, from Buxtehude's use of the feet in pedal solos, which unlocked the power of an organ's largest pipes, to his exploitation of the height and breadth of a space through multiple musicians playing in the galleries, to his introduction of church concerts untethered to religious services and ceremonies, there must have been something particularly striking to Bach about Buxtehude's freedom to direct, develop and experiment with his art. The independence and liberation of Buxtehude's position must have made a great impression. Lübeck's free status, its wealth and cosmopolitan outlook meant that the Marienkirche's musical director enjoyed an autonomy that must have seemed revelatory to the young man from Thuringia, hemmed in as his family's careers had been by church consistories, town councils and provincial courts. To a student, fan or acolyte, what an artist produces is the draw, but how he or she goes about it is a fascination. Buxtehude's versatility and free-thinking were surely powerful fuels to Bach's inner fires: if, on his outward journey, he had mulled over where he had come from and what he hoped to learn, his return would have been propelled by ideas about what he wanted to be, how he wanted to live and what he would write and practise in order to get there.

Scholars detect the echo of Buxtehude's thought and techniques in a wide arc of Bach's work. Going beyond conventional formulae, Peter Williams writes, 'In both choral and organ music,' Buxtehude created 'winsome and new melodies out of the old hymn-tunes, weaving them around with ornamental gestures typical of sophisticated paraphrasing techniques.' Williams believes Bach copied four organ ostinati and took them back to Arnstadt, and later responded to them with his Passacaglia in C minor for Organ, BWV 582, 'by taking the idea so much further, i.e. searching for greater length and development.' Other researchers see the same spectacle, Bach rapidly assimilating and transcending Buxtehude's influence. American musicologist David Yearsley writes of Buxtehude's compositions for organ that 'the feet do not elaborate the theme; they are dependable, if seemingly uncreative. Bach's passacaglia sets itself free of these constraints.' Bach, Yearsley asserts, 'explodes the generic guidelines he brought back with him from Lübeck.' Philipp Spitta sees 'reminiscences' of Buxtehude in the prelude of Bach's Fugue in A minor, a work in which Spitta hears 'science and effect united in the most perfect manner'.

The fugue begins in quiet and ascends, while seeming to fall and gather like water, to a resonant and shivering might. It might well make a theme for Bach's walk, and the abandonment of the timid and pedestrian musical horizons of Arnstadt for the rushing possibilities and futures suggested by what he found in Lübeck.

We feel giddy and euphoric as we finish recording our discoveries in the Marienkirche. Lindsay is delighted, Richard is happy that he has captured all we have encountered, and I am both joyful and unreconciled: I would like to carry on, to follow this spirit further, to understand more of his life and craft.

Richard wants to experiment with a new arrangement of microphones and to this end has brought with him the polystyrene head of a mannequin with a mic taped over each ear. Solemnly and sedately, he parades it around the church; as if conducting some bizarre rite of his own, he paces through a huddle of people who are taking part in their own ritual. Incomprehension and amazement are writ large across their expressions as Richard circles the nave. Lindsay has a fit of giggles.

The end of the expedition is a meal, more subdued than any we have had so far, and loading the car, and a drive to Hamburg airport. We save and swap audio and picture files, and sort ourselves out, and hug and say farewell and catch our planes home. Lindsay cuts five days of audio down to five programmes, beautifully shaped, crafted and illustrated with Bach's music. Broadcast on Radio 3 in the run-up to Christmas, they are a success.

Of all the messages I received there is one I treasure particularly, from a renowned playwright whom I have never met. He wrote of his susceptibility to 'a deep weird depression' before Christmas, and of the comfort listening to the walks gave him: 'There was a quality of attentiveness, vitality and indeed love,' he wrote. 'I felt I was with you on that walk and it really lifted my soul.' The privilege of walking with him, and a great many unknown listeners, and with Richard and Lindsay particularly, and with Bach's spirit, above all, was deep indeed, and my motivation for telling this story.

Parting from Bach in the Marienkirche, at the start of what must have been transformative months in Lübeck, seems the right place to take leave from him. His return journey through the cold in early 1706, back to face reprimands of Arnstadt, must have been quite different, powered by resolution, perhaps, more than anticipation. No wonder his job there did not last much longer: in April of the following year he auditioned for the post of organist at the Divi-Blasii-Kirche in Mühlhausen, to which he was appointed in June.

No wonder he answered the consistory court in Arnstadt as he did, brusquely, haughtily and defiantly. He had been changed by his journeys and his discoveries. He would not be held back now, and perhaps deep down he knew – or anyway, was surely much closer to knowing – that his music would never be silenced. His most impassioned biographer, John Eliot Gardiner, identifies a quality of Bach's work that speaks to us most clearly and powerfully: the sense of certainty, 'his belief that somewhere there exists a path leading to a harmonious existence, if not in this world then in the next.'

Acknowledgements

This book began life as *Bach Walks*, a documentary series on BBC Radio 3, and huge thanks must go to Alan Davey, controller of Radio 3, who commissioned the programme and was also the originator of *Sound Walks* – listeners to and creators of radio (and slow radio in particular) are in his debt. The first in the series was produced by Philip Tagney; great thanks to him, and to Peter Florence and Becky Shaw, who suggested that I might be the presenter Philip needed.

The *Bach Walks* were wonderfully conceived, directed and produced by Lindsay Kemp: having done a recce, our walk and a subsequent tour, Lindsay is probably the world's leading expert on Bach's journey. I cannot thank him enough for his knowledge, his guidance and his kindness in giving the manuscript a marvellously thorough read.

No sound walk would sound nearly as good as they do without the immense skill, patience and endurance of Richard Andrews, as fine a sound recordist as exists anywhere, and, like Lindsay and Philip, a delightful travelling companion.

We were overseen by our editor Jessica Isaacs and Edward Blakeman, commissioner and Head of Music at BBC Radio 3, who also kindly supported the publishing of this book with Little Toller. Many thanks indeed to them both, and to Matthew Dodd, and before him Abigail Appleton, current and former heads of speech: friends and mentors for whom it has been my great pleasure to work over the years.

I am deeply grateful to Ed Kluz for his gorgeous artwork, and to Adrian and Gracie Cooper, Graham Shackleton and Jon Woolcott at Little Toller, whose beautiful books are treasures, and whose support, wit, expertise and sympathy are blessings to their authors. Thank you!

My agent, Zoe Waldie, and her assistant, Miriam Tobin, are unfailingly supportive and superb. Thank you both.

John Clare gave me my first taste of Bach, and this manuscript his attention. Thank you, dearest Dad, and thank you, dearest Sally and Alexander Clare.

At home: Rebecca, Aubrey, Robin, Jennifer and Gerald make all my travels possible. My deepest love and thanks to you all.

H. C.
Hebden Bridge, 2018

Little Toller Books

We publish old and new writing attuned to nature and the landscape, working with a wide range of the very best writers and artists. We pride ourselves on publishing affordable books of the highest quality. If you have enjoyed this book, you will also like exploring our other titles.

Anthology
ARBOREAL: WOODLAND WORDS
CORNERSTONES: SUBTERRANEAN WRITING

Field Notes
MY HOUSE OF SKY: THE LIFE OF J. A. BAKER *Hetty Saunders*
DEER ISLAND *Neil Ansell*
ORISON FOR A CURLEW *Horatio Clare*
LOVE, MADNESS, FISHING *Dexter Petley*
WATER AND SKY *Neil Sentance*
THE TREE *John Fowles*

New Nature Monographs
HERBACEOUS *Paul Evans*
ON SILBURY HILL *Adam Thorpe*
THE ASH TREE *Oliver Rackham*
MERMAIDS *Sophia Kingshill*
BLACK APPLES OF GOWER *Iain Sinclair*
BEYOND THE FELL WALL *Richard Skelton*
LIMESTONE COUNTRY *Fiona Sampson*
HAVERGEY *John Burnside*
SNOW *Marcus Sedgwick*
LANDFILL *Tim Dee*
SPIRITS OF PLACE *Sara Maitland*

Nature Classics Library
THROUGH THE WOODS *H.E. Bates*
MEN AND THE FIELDS *Adrian Bell*
THE MIRROR OF THE SEA *Joseph Conrad*
ISLAND YEARS, ISLAND FARM *Frank Fraser Darling*
THE MAKING OF THE ENGLISH LANDSCAPE *W. G. Hoskins*
BROTHER TO THE OX *Fred Kitchen*
FOUR HEDGES *Clare Leighton*
DREAM ISLAND *R. M. Lockley*
THE UNOFFICIAL COUNTRYSIDE *Richard Mabey*
RING OF BRIGHT WATER *Gavin Maxwell*
EARTH MEMORIES *Llewelyn Powys*
IN PURSUIT OF SPRING *Edward Thomas*
THE NATURAL HISTORY OF SELBORNE *Gilbert White*

LITTLE TOLLER BOOKS
Lower Dairy, Toller Fratrum, Dorset DT2 oEL
W. littletoller.co.uk **E.** books@littletoller.co.uk